HANDICRAFT GIFTS

HANDICRAFT GIFTS

Eve Harlow

Sundial

Contents

Introduction 6

Needlework 8

Miniature dolls 8
Patchwork coverlet 10
Clamshell teacosy 12
Smocking 14
Baby basket 16
Daisy Mae rag doll 18
Embroidered apron 20
Canvaswork pincushion 22
Handkerchief gifts 24
Sewing box 26

Flowers and herbs 28

Immortelles 28
Pressed flowers 30
Sweet-smelling gifts from flowers and herbs 32

Paint Jobs 36

Roses all the way 36
Decorating with paints 38
Decorating with stencils 42
Pictures on stones 44
Owls and elephants 46

Wood Crafts 48

How-tall-am-I measure 48
Spice and herb jar rack 50
Doll's cradle 52

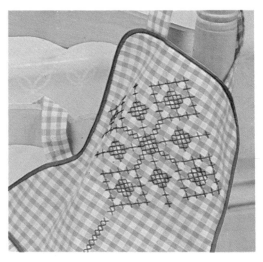

First published in 1978 by
Sundial Books Limited
59 Grosvenor Street, London W1.
© 1978 Hennerwood Publications
Limited

ISBN 0 904230 07 8

Printed in England by
Severn Valley Press Limited

Felt and Fabric 55

Bags of money! 54
Thimble pips 55
Pencil holders 56
Ribbon cushions 58
Covered matchboxes 60
Doorstep cat 62
Leather gifts 64
Map case 66
Car wash mitt 67
Sleepy dog toy 68
Pyjama case bunny 70
Dressing table set 72

Papercrafts 74

Jewelled tree 77
The art of découpage 78
Papier mâché 80
Handmade cards 82
All wrapped up 84

Knitting and Crochet 86

Lacy wool shawl 86
Sweet Sue 88
Knitted elephant 90

Children only 92

Gifts for older children
to make 94

Index 96

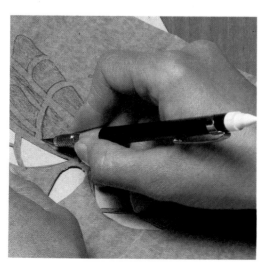

Introduction

Handicraft Gifts is a book for the whole family. Keep it by you the whole year round as a source of ideas for gifts you can make for family and friends. All of the gift ideas involve handicrafts, some of which you will know, but others may be new to you. This book not only gives you the opportunity of making gifts that are original, but also enables you to try out new handicrafts.

Some of the gift ideas are quick-makes, easy and inexpensive gifts for all occasions. These makes will also be particularly useful for bazaars and fund-raising events.

Other gifts take time and trouble to make properly. These are the gifts you will like to give on special occasions, and which will be treasured for years to come.

In the sewing chapter, there are things to make using a variety of needlecrafts — smocking, patchwork, box making, canvaswork and so on — and instructions for making a charming rag doll. *Felt and fabric craft* has ideas for making things with felt — moneybags for children's money gifts, thimble pips, pencil cases and desk sets, as well as some bright ideas for presents for homemakers and for brides.

Men are not forgotten; there are superb leather gifts to make for fathers, husbands, brothers, uncles and grandfathers. And for those who like making soft toys, there is a pattern for a sleepy dog toy that makes one feel sleepy just to look at it!

Flower crafts, which are becoming more and more popular with country people and town people alike, includes preserving whole flowers for making 'immortelle' arrangements, preserving petals and herbs for perfume sachets and sleep pillows, and ways of pressing flowers and leaves for picture making.

Paint jobs is a chapter of ideas for everyone who likes to work with paint. Even if you cannot draw a straight line, there are ideas you can use for decorating all kinds of things. Old enamel pots and jugs can be turned into brilliant, colourful bargeware. Big beach stones make pretty paperweights and mementoes. Boxes and tins will make attractive containers for biscuits and sweets.

Woodcrafts is a chapter for both men and women. Even if you have never tried to knock in a nail you will find the instructions for making the rocker cradle and the spice rack very easy and straightforward.

Papercrafts shows you a number of ways of making gifts from various kinds of paper. Fascinating handicrafts, such as papier mâché and decoupage are explained and you will find many ways of using the basic techniques to make a wide variety of gifts. This chapter also provides you with ideas for making your own gift cards and for wrapping gifts in the prettiest ways.

For those who like to make knitted and crocheted gifts, there are three delightful patterns: a shawl to crochet that might well become a family heirloom, an amusing pink elephant to knit, and Sweet Sue, a doll to sit on the shelf, full of sweets.

Finally, for children, there are four whole pages of ideas for gifts they can make for mothers and fathers, for relatives and for friends. Some of the gifts are simple and suitable for children up to seven or eight years old to make. Others are a little more complex and are more suitable for children up to thirteen or fourteen years old.

However, older children will be able to find ideas for presents and gifts throughout this book. Although most older children are used to using scissors and crafts' knives at school, do keep an eye on them when these tools are recommended in the list of tools required. Similarly, keep a watchful eye on glues and adhesives. Some adhesives, such as rubber solution, should not be used in rooms with poor ventilation or where there is a naked flame. Other adhesives will mark clothes and furnishings if they are spilled or used carelessly.

Following patterns

Measurements You will see that throughout this book, both imperial and metric measurements are given. This is because some people find it easier to work in inches and feet. Others, children for instance, are already quite comfortable in metric measures. Work with whichever set of measurements suits you best, but do not try and convert one to the other.

Graph patterns You will see that some of the projects in this book are made using graph patterns. Do not be put off from using these patterns. They are not difficult to work with. They do take a little time to draw out but the end result is so worth while. Use squared pattern paper if you can obtain it. Most large stores and shops sell it in the dressmaking or haberdashery departments. If you cannot obtain pattern paper easily, draw out your own squares on tracing paper or kitchen greaseproof paper.

How to use the book

When you are thinking about a gift, look through the book. Think about the handicrafts you can already do. See if any of the ideas on these pages appeal to you. Perhaps something will start you thinking about a design you would like to try. Consider the handicrafts which are new to you and read through the basic techniques.

Gifts for children When you are making gifts for children, whether toys or things to wear, keep the safety factor in mind. Use non-inflammable fabrics and, if you are making toys with features, sew on eyes, mouths etc., very carefully so that they cannot be pulled — or chewed — off. Stuffings for soft toys should be washable if possible so that toys can be kept clean. Wooden toys should be finished off smoothly, without corners, splintery surfaces or nails or screws protruding. Enamel paints should be used for decoration or, if water based paints are used, finish the surface with polyurethane varnish.

Motifs On pages 40-41, some motifs are provided for you to use as decorations on your handmade gifts. These are to help you to make your own designs. You can use the motifs for embroidery, for canvaswork, for appliqué, for stencilling, for painting and for making gift cards and printing gift wraps. Trace them off and use them full size. If you want to make the motifs larger or smaller, here is how it is done. Trace the motif from the page. Draw a box round it, touching the edges. Decide the size you want to draw it. Draw a box to this size. Now divide both boxes into squares with pencilled lines. Then, copy the lines of the motif from one squared box to the other. You will soon find this technique quite simple.

You are going to have a lot of fun with handicraft gifts — and you will give a lot of pleasure too.

Needlework

Decorative needlework is one of the pleasantest ways of making gifts for your family and your friends. It is not a quick way of making things — sewing takes time and patience, as well as skill.

But your own hand-made gifts will have an individual quality not found in commercially made goods, which will be cherished by those who receive them. The knowledge of the time and careful work you have devoted to them will give these gifts a special meaning.

In this chapter, the crafts include patchwork, smocking, embroidery, canvaswork and doll-making with some unusual ideas for sewing pretty gifts from ordinary pocket handkerchiefs.

Miniature dolls

Making miniature dolls from clothes pegs was a popular handicraft for girls 100 years ago. The little figures were exquisitely dressed in silks, satins and cambrics, lavishly trimmed with lace. Tiny hats were topped with a dyed feather or the dolls wore crowns or tiaras made of crystals and pearl beads. The art lay in the detail put into the design of the costume and the fine sewing that was used to sew the clothes.

When dolly pegs were replaced by snap clothes pegs, the craft was almost forgotten. Nowadays, dolly pegs are available again and this delightful sewing craft is enjoying a revival.

Features Draw the features on the doll first. Keep them as simple as possible. You will probably find that you need little more than fairly large eyes and, perhaps, a tiny mouth. Brush one coat of varnish over the drawn features and leave to dry.

Making the arms Wind a pipe cleaner around the peg at shoulder height. Cross the ends at the back and secure with a few stitches. Cut thin strips of tissue to cover the arms. Spread a little glue along the pipe cleaner arms and wind the tissues neatly from shoulder to the hand. Glue the ends down firmly (*see diagram 1*).

Dressing the doll Every part of the costume is stitched together. Do not use glue anywhere. After a while, glue seeps through fine fabrics.

☐ BODICE For the bodice, cut a piece of the dress fabric 5cm (2in) square. Turn a narrow hem on one edge and stitch. Fold the fabric around the peg. Turn in the raw edges and stitch sides together firmly down the back. Work some long stitches in matching thread over the top of the arms to keep the bodice in place (*see diagram 2*).

☐ PETTICOAT Decide where the waist of the doll will be. A highwaisted fashion will need the waist in a different place from that on a doll dressed, for instance, in Elizabethan costume. Measure the distance from the waist to the bottom of the peg. Cut a piece of Vilene about 10cm (4in) wide and to the depth required. (For some costumes you may want the petticoat fuller. If so, cut it wider than 10cm (4in).)

Sew the back seam of the petticoat. Work small gathering stitches around the waist. Put the petticoat on the doll, draw up the gathering stitches and then sew the petticoat to the dress bodice. The doll will now stand up.

☐ SKIRT Cut the fabric for the skirt of the dress. It is made in the same way as the petticoat but has more fabric in the width. Make a tiny, neat hem on one long edge. Sew on lace or other trimmings at this stage. Gather the waist and fit on the doll. Sew the skirt to the bodice.

☐ SLEEVES Measure and cut strips of fabric for the sleeves. Sew the long sides together to make tubes of fabric. Put the sleeves on the arms. Turn in a hem at the shoulder and neatly hem the sleeves to the bodice.

☐ TRIMMINGS Whatever details you add to the dress, collars, ruffs, cuffs etc., must be made just as you would make them for a dress for yourself. There should not be raw edges anywhere. Seams must be narrow and stitches almost invisible.

☐ HAIR STYLES Spread glue on the head and wind the yarn round to make the hairstyle. If the style is bouffant, spread more glue and pile more yarn where it is needed. Buns, 'ear-phones', chignons etc., should be made in the hand and afterwards stitched to the head. To make ringlets, double a length of yarn, twist it tightly and then double it again. Sew ringlets to the hair.

☐ HATS AND HEADDRESSES Hats can be made of Vilene which is stiff enough to hold a shape. Make mob caps from muslin. Ribbon or braid can be used as a base for headdresses.

Miniature dolls

Materials required

Dolly pegs
Good quality pipe cleaners
Medium-weight Vilene
Clear all-purpose adhesive
Fabrics for clothes: these should be
   very light in weight: thin cotton,
   lawn, muslin, silk, soft net etc.
Sewing threads to match fabrics
Knitting yarn for hair, brown,
   yellow, grey, white, black
Trims: narrow ribbons and lace,
   braids, beads, tiny buttons
Pink or peach coloured paper
   tissues
Felt-tipped pens or water colours
Clear varnish

Tools you will need

Pins
Needles, the finest you can
   manage to use
Scissors for cutting fabrics
Small scissors for trimming
Tape measure
Brush for varnish

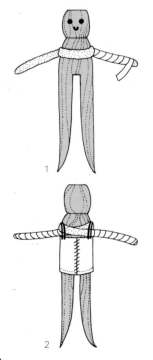

Patchwork coverlet

Patchwork coverlet

Materials required

Base fabric: calico or cotton 90cm × 60cm (36in × 24in)

Backing and frill: choose a plain cotton, 1½m (1½yd)

If using ribbon for the frill (see below) you will need 1m (1yd) of fabric and 6m (6yd) of wide ribbon

Patchwork fabrics: cotton and cotton mixtures

Terylene wadding for interlining (optional)

Sewing threads

Embroidery threads

Tools you will need

Sewing needle
Embroidery needle
Pins
Scissors
Sewing machine (optional)

Here is a gift to sew for a new baby. Even if you have never before attempted patchwork you will find crazy patchwork quite easy to do. No templates are needed and you can finish the patchwork by hand or using a sewing machine.

Patchwork is traditionally a re-cycling craft using pieces of fabric cut from cast-off clothing or dressmaking remnants. If you already have suitable fabric scraps in pretty, toning colours and prints, by all means use them. Otherwise, buy new cotton fabrics in 10cm (4in) lengths. You will find that fabric counters in large stores are quite used to supplying short lengths for patchworkers! Choose only cotton or cotton mixture fabrics for patchwork items which are going to need frequent laundering, such as the coverlet. Do not mix fabric weights. The heavy fabric will pull away from the lighter. Make sure that all the fabrics you use are colour-fast and pre-shrunk. For this reason, it is a wise precaution to wash and iron all patchwork fabrics before you use them. It would be a pity if all your careful work were wasted just because you used fabrics which shrank or which ran in the wash.

The quantity of fabrics given are for making a frilled coverlet about 90cm × 60cm (36in × 24in). The quantities can be adapted to make bed-sized quilts. The technique is basically the same.

Preparing the patchwork Cut the base fabric to size and spread it on the table top. Cut the first patch for the top, left hand corner. Cut it to fit the corner and leave the edge 'crazy'. Pin and then baste the patch to the base fabric leaving the crazy edge free. Choose and cut patch 2 to any shape or size. Slip one edge under the basted-down patch. Cut the top edge straight. Pin and baste, leaving the crazy edge free (*diagram 1*). Continue adding patches (*diagram 2*) until the whole of the base fabric has been covered. Choose any of the methods which are listed below under *Sewing crazy patchwork* to complete the patchwork.

Sewing crazy patchwork Choose any of the following methods to sew crazy patchwork.

□ HAND SEWING Using a fine needle and matching threads, turn a narrow seam hem on the crazy edges of the patches. Work small hemming stitches or slip stitches. Afterwards, if you like, cover the edges with embroidery stitches. You might also decide to embroider over some of the plain-coloured patches for textural contrast. (See illustration)

□ HAND SEWING — METHOD 2 This is the traditional method for working crazy patchwork. Work small running stitches along the raw edges of the patchwork. Remove the basting and then work chunky embroidery stitches over the running stitches and covering the raw edges.

□ MACHINE SEWING — METHOD 1 This technique can be worked with a straight-stitch machine. Set the machine to a fairly large stitch. Stitch along all the raw edges of the patches, about 3mm (⅛in) from the edge. Embroider over the stitching afterwards.

□ MACHINE-WORKED EMBROIDERY This technique can only be worked with a swing-needle machine. Set the machine to work a narrow satin stitch. Work along all the raw edges. You might change the thread colour occasionally for effect. If you have a fully automatic machine, you can choose from the variety of embroidery stitches the machine will do, to cover the raw edges of the patches.

Making an interlining The coverlet can be interlined with wadding, or not, as you prefer. If you decide to interline, cut the wadding to the same size as the patchwork and baste to the wrong side. Cut the backing fabric also to the same size as the patchwork.

Making the frill Cut the remaining fabric into strips 87mm (3½in) wide. Join strips to make a long band 6m (6yd) long. Neaten one long edge either by working a hem with the sewing machine hemming attachment or by working a small, tight zigzag stitch on the edge, afterwards trimming away the fabric up to the stitches. (If you are making the coverlet by hand, it would be better to use a wide ribbon instead of making a frill. See under *Materials required* for the amounts of ribbon and backing fabric needed.)

Making the coverlet Gather the frill to fit round the edges of the coverlet. Seam the short ends together. Pin and baste the frill to the right side of the patchwork, raw edges together and right sides facing. Lay the backing fabric on top, right side downwards. Machine-stitch all round with 12mm (½in) seams leaving 15cm (6in) unstitched in the middle of one seam for turning the coverlet. Trim the seam allowances. Turn the coverlet to the right side. Close the seam with slip stitches.

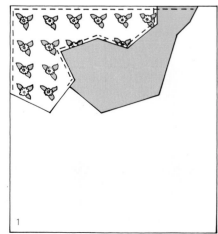

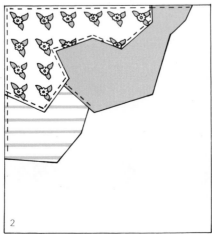

Clamshell teacosy

Clamshell teacosy

Materials required

For a similar cosy, 4 fabric colours,
   25cm (10in) of each colour, 90cm
   (1yd) wide fabric.
Terylene wadding
Plain cotton fabric for lining and
   backing, 90cm (1yd)
Piping cord 1.5m (1½yd)
Card, paper for templates
Matching sewing threads
Basting thread

Tools you will need

Sharp scissors
Ruler, pencil
Dressmaker pins
Fine sewing needle
Piece of cork for working surface
   (or table with folded blanket and
   clean sheet on top)

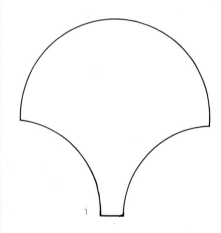

Clamshell patchwork is different from traditional patchwork in that the stitching is done from the right side — rather as appliqué is worked. Clamshell patchwork is absorbing to do and you should always allow sufficient time to complete a row of shapes at one sitting.

The template Clamshell templates can be bought from needlework shops and counters but if it is difficult for you to buy patchwork accessories, trace off the clamshell shape provided (*diagram 1*) and use it to make an accurate template of stiff cardboard. Use the card template to cut all your papers and patches. It is essential for success that the paper shapes be cleanly and accurately cut.

Papers As for traditional patchwork, the fabric is cut out to shape and then mounted on a paper shape. The papers are left until the patchwork is finished. Thin, stiff paper is best — such as good notepaper or brown paper. Gift cards can also be cut up.

Fabrics Fabrics for all traditional patchwork should be smooth, fairly fine and closely woven. For clamshell patchwork, smooth, fine fabric is essential. Cotton, cotton and polyester mixtures or silk are the best fabrics to use for the teacosy.

Preparing the fabric Press all the creases out of the fabrics. Lay the master template on the wrong side of the fabric and pencil round. Mark the position of each clamshell 18mm (¾in) apart to allow for seam allowances. The grain of the fabric must always run down the patch.

Preparing the patches Cut out the paper clamshells. Cut out the fabric clamshells with 9mm (⅜in) seam allowance on the curve only. The stem of the clamshell is cut without a seam allowance. Lay a paper shape on the wrong side of the fabric shape and pin together. Turn the seam allowance onto the paper and baste. The curves must be kept smooth and without bumps so, to mount the fabric, you must make tiny pleats, the basting stitches holding the pleats down. If it does not look right, unpick and baste again because you can never hide a badly made clamshell in sewing. Remove the holding pins and dry-press all the clamshells from the wrong side.

To start the teacosy Make 68 clamshells. You need more than you can actually see in the illustrated teacosy because there have to be 2 extra clamshells in some rows for seam allowance. You will need 12 of the lightest tone, 12 of the next colour, 17 of the next deepest and 27 of the deepest shade.

Sewing the patchwork Clamshell patchwork is started from the top. Lay 3 white clamshells in a row, the sides touching right sides up. Lay a ruler across the top. Lay 4 white clamshells for row 2, the curves overlapping the raw edges of row 1. Use pins to hold the patches in position while you baste the two rows together.

To sew, start on the right, and with tiny hemming stitches sew round the curves of row 2, stitching the clamshells to those in row 1. Unpick the basting threads, holding the rows together. (The basting holding the papers is left until the end.) Dry-press on the wrong side and re-lay for row 3. *Diagram 3* shows how many patches and which colours are in each row. (Row 3 has 5 white patches, row 4 has 6 pale colour patches, and so on.)

Continue basting, hemming, removing basting, pressing each row until you have stitched all the clamshells.

Making up the teacosy Give the patchwork a final pressing from the wrong side and cut the basting threads holding the papers. Shake the papers out. (Keep them, you can use them again.) Trim the edges of the patchwork to shape, leaving 12mm (½in) seam allowance all round. Cut the cosy backing to the same shape. Prepare the piping and baste it along the seam allowance line of the cosy back, but not along the

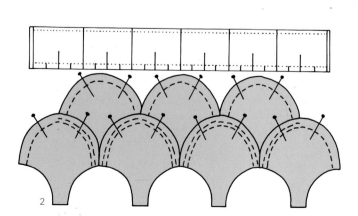

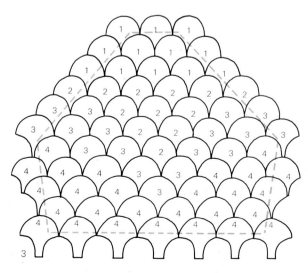

bottom edge. Machine stitch, using a piping foot. Remove basting. Baste the patchwork, right side down, to the right side of the cosy back. Machine stitch from the backing side, so that you can stitch over the previous stitching line. Pin and baste piping cord to the right side of the bottom edges of the cosy. Machine stitch.
Lining the cosy Cut 2 wadding pieces to the exact size of the cosy, without seam allowances.

Overstitch the pieces together, leaving the bottom open. Put into the cosy cover.

Cut two lining pieces to the same size as the cosy with 12mm seam allowances. Machine stitch the lining pieces together. Trim the seam allowance and slip the lining inside the cosy. Turn up the bottom edge of the lining and slip-stitch the outer fabric and lining together to finish.

Smocking

Smocking and embroidery stitches

Smocking is embroidery worked on gathered fabric and was once used mainly on babies' and children's clothes. Modern embroidery design uses smocking not only for gathering fabric but also as a decoration on all kinds of clothes and accessories. While a great many embroidery stitches can be used for smocking, in fact three basic stitches are all one really needs. These are stem stitch, cable stitch and honeycomb stitch. If you think of these three stitches as having different degrees of control, you will always know where to use them. On the needlebook cover illustrated, the smocking uses only one stitch — cable stitch. The workbox uses two stitches, cable stitch and honeycomb stitch.

☐ CABLE STITCH It is worked in a similar way to stem stitch but the thread is laid first on one side of the needle and then on the other, alternately. Cable stitch can be worked in rows to make a band. This has a medium hold and is looser than stem stitch.

☐ HONEYCOMB STITCH The diagram shows how the stitch is worked. As a surface stitch, it is called Chevron stitch. This is the loosest of the three basic stitches and is therefore often used at the bottom of a piece of smocking so that the fabric can flare. Honeycomb stitch has quite a lot of stretch in it. Worked across three rows of gathers, honeycomb becomes vandyke stitch.

Preparing the fabric The most important rule in smocking is accurate and uniform gathering. Transfer dots can be purchased from needle-work shops and counters and these are ironed onto the wrong side of the fabric. The dots are picked up with the needle and gathering thread. However, the easiest fabric for a beginner to practise on is a checked cotton fabric, or a stripe or spot pattern. Transfer dots are then not needed.

How to gather As a rough guide, smocking reduces the width of fabric to one-third of the original, so cut fabric to three times the finished width required. If the fabric is plain, transfer dots to the wrong side of the fabric. If you are using a patterned fabric, plan which dot or line you will pick up across the width. Thread a fine sewing needle with strong cotton thread in a bright, contrasting colour, a few centimetres (inches) longer than the width of the fabric. Knot the end. Work from right to left and make a small backstitch to secure the knot. Pass the needle in and out of the fabric taking stitches of even length, passing the needle under each transferred dot (or line of check). At the end, leave the thread hanging and slip the needle off. Work a second row about 8mm ($5/16$in) away, and as many rows of gathering as required in the same way. Finally, gather all the thread ends in one hand and 'stroke' the gathers back towards the knots. Move the gathers back as far as they will go easily. Then, pull each thread gently until the gathers lie straight, side by side. The gathers in the fabric are called 'reeds'. Do not cut any of the threads off. Wind pairs of threads around vertically inserted pins, in a figure-of-eight and adjust the reeds so that you can just see the gathering threads between them.

Finishing smocking off After smocking has been completed, cut the gathering threads away from the pins and take out the pins. Pull the gathering stitches out gently from the knot end.

Warning: never remove gathering stitches while you are working a piece to see how it is getting on. You will never be able to regather it.

Fabrics and threads Cotton is the best and

Work box

Materials required

Cotton fabric for outside 76cm × 90cm (30in × 36in)
Lining fabric 36cm × 120cm (15in × 48in)
Stiff card 30cm × 45cm (12in × 18in)
Wadding 15cm × 15cm (6in × 6in)
4 paper fasteners
Clear all-purpose adhesive
Gathering thread
Embroidery thread

Needlebook

Materials required

Patterned cotton fabric 69cm × 18cm (28in × 7in) for the outside and the same fabric, 23cm × 17cm (9in × 6¾in) for the inside.
Thin card, two pieces 16cm × 11cm (6¼in × 4¼in)
Embroidery thread, 1 skein, colour picked from the fabric pattern
Gathering thread
Curtain ring 25mm (1in)
Heavy weight Vilene for inside pages
Clear, all-purpose adhesive

Tools you will need

Scissors
Pinking shears
Fine needle
Pins

easiest fabric for smocking. Shantung, voile, crêpe de Chine, linen, gingham and similar woven fabrics can also be used but it is better to leave the finer fabrics until you are more experienced.

□ THREADS Choose a thread of a similar thickness to the fabric itself. For fine cotton and silk, two strands of stranded embroidery thread are sufficient. No. 8 Perle looks very well on denim or Vyella fabric. Coton-a-broder has an attractive, dull finish. Generally smocking looks best in a single colour or, at the most, two colours.

Needlebook

To make the cover Lay the lining piece wrong side up on the table and lay the two pieces of card, touching, 6mm (¼in) from the fabric edges. Cut the corners of the fabric off diagonally and turn the edges onto the card, glueing them down. Leave to dry and do the smocking.

Work rows of gathering stitch across the width of the cover fabric, starting 12mm (½in) from the top edge. Work the gathering 12mm (½in) from each side of the fabric, so that you leave a margin for turning a hem later.

The rows of gathering should be 8mm (⁵/₁₆in) apart, but you may be guided by the lines of a check if you are using a checked fabric.

On the needlebook illustrated, cable stitch was worked in rows of two, 10mm (³/₈in) apart, with 18mm (¾in) between the double rows. The last row of smocking should be 12mm (½in) from the bottom edge. Remove gathering stitches.

Making up the needlebook Baste the turnings on the smocked cover and slip stitch to the needlebook lining. Cut pages from the Vilene using pinking shears. Backstitch inside the book. For a decoration, cover a curtain ring with close buttonhole stitch and make small tassel. Stitch to the cover.

Smocked work box

This is a different type of stitched fabric box. It has handles for carrying and has a smocked skirt. The skirt uses only two smocking stitches, cable stitch and honeycomb. A row of feather stitch is used for decoration round the hem.

To make the box The box illustrated has sides 150mm (6in) deep and 131mm (5¼in) wide.

Make the sides first.

Cut four pieces of stiff card 150mm × 133mm (6in × 5¼in). Cut four pieces of lining fabric to the same size plus 6mm (¼in) seam allowance all round. Cut the corners off diagonally and mount on the wrong side, glueing the edges.

Sew the four box sides together with oversewing stitches, the lined side to the inside.

Cut a box base 131mm × 131mm (5¼in × 5¼in). Cover with fabric in the same way, but interlining a piece of wadding between the fabric and the card.

Cut a strip of lining fabric to the depth of the box plus 25mm (1in) and to the circumference plus 25mm (1in).

Turn a hem on the top edge and glue. Wrap round the box and overlap the ends. Stitch with slip stitches.

Turn the bottom hem onto the bottom of the box and glue. Cut a piece of card for the outer bottom and mount fabric on it. Push four paper fasteners through from the card side. Open the prongs. The fasteners make small brass feet for the box. Glue the outer base to the box bottom.

Cut a strip of fabric 30cm (12in) long and 50mm (2in) wide. Turn narrow hems on the long sides and then turn again to the middle. Slip stitch the seams. Press.

Sew the strip to opposite corners of the box.

To make the smocked skirt Make up a strip of fabric for the skirt, three times the circumference of the box plus 25mm (1in). Turn a hem on the top edge, 12mm (½in) and gather through both thicknesses. Work four rows of gathering. Work two rows of cable stitch and one row of honeycombing. Remove the gathering stitches and join the short ends of the strip to fit around the box. Work featherstitching down the seam and down the other three corners to match.

Turn up the hem and work feather stitching round. Stitch the skirt around the box top.

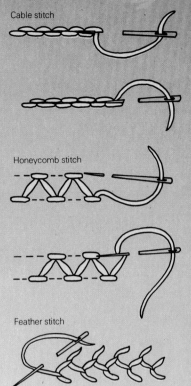

Cable stitch

Honeycomb stitch

Feather stitch

Cable stitch *This stitch is worked from left to right. Bring the needle through on the line of the design. Insert the point to the right on the line and bring the point out midway on the length of the stitch (a) with the thread below the needle. Work the next stitch in the same way but with the thread above the needle.*

In smocking, the thread is taken over two reeds and then picks up one reed.

Honeycomb stitch *Bring the needle through on the lower line on the left. Insert the needle a little to the right and take a small stitch, the point of the needle emerging halfway along the stitch being made. Now take the needle to the upper line a little to the right and draw through to the wrong side. Bring it out again to the left and make a small stitch as before, emerging at the centre. Work in this way, alternating on the lower and upper lines.*

In smocking, work from left to right in the same way, bringing the needle out to the left of a reed, take the thread over two reeds and pick up one reed, the needle coming out between the reeds.

Feather stitch *Bring needle out at top centre, hold thread down with left thumb, insert needle a little to the right on same level and take a small stitch down to centre, keeping thread under needle point. Next, insert needle a little to the left on same level and take a stitch to centre, keeping thread under needle point. Work these two movements alternately.*

RIGHT: *Drawing up the gathering stitches to form the reeds for smocking*

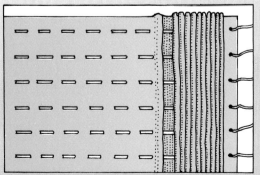

Baby basket

This pretty frilled basket would make a lovely gift for a mother who has a new baby. Baby baskets are filled with baby toiletries — powder, cream, baby oil, cotton wool buds and balls, spare nappy pins and so on and the basket can be carried on the arm easily. The base of the baby basket is an ordinary wooden fruit basket, the kind that fruiterers supply strawberries in.

Making the pattern Measure the dimensions of the basket and make paper patterns of the sides and base. Call the base A, the long side B and the short side C.

Lining the basket Cut a strip of the quilted fabric to line the basket sides. You will need twice the length of the long side, twice the length of the short side plus 25mm (1in) for overlap, by the depth. Spread a little glue round the inside top edge and round the bottom sides and press the quilting into the basket, turning under and glueing the ends in a corner. Using the paper pattern A, cut a piece of quilting for the bottom of the basket, adding about 12mm (½in) all round. Turn the cut edges under and glue the quilting to the bottom of the basket. Cut a strip and a base of the same quilting fabric to cover the outside of the basket. Turn in the top edges and draw them together with tiny oversewing stitches. Make the lining next.

Use the paper patterns to cut the pieces. You will need one A, two B's and two C's. Add 12mm (½in) seam allowance all round each piece as you cut out. Stitch the five pieces together to make a basket lining. Trim the seam allowances. Fit the lining into the basket and turn a narrow hem on the top edge. Pin it in position. Make an outer cover for the basket using the same paper patterns but this time, add 25mm (1in) all round to allow for the padding. Fit the cover on and turn a hem on the top edge.

Oversew the top edges together neatly.

Covering the handle Pad the handle of the basket with a strip of cotton wool, catching it together with big basting stitches. Cut a piece of cotton fabric to cover the wool, making the seam on the underside of the handle.

Cut two pieces of lace to fit the handle and machine stitch them together. Wrap the lace round the handle so that the seam is on the underside and slipstitch the two edges on top to the cotton fabric.

Making the frill Fold the Terylene fabric in half along its length and baste the two layers together. Try the piece around the basket, overlapping the ends about 25mm (1in). Cut off the excess fabric. Cut pieces of frilling to the same length and then pieces of lace to the same length. Machine stitch the lace to the top edge of the frilling. Pin and baste the frilling in rows to the Terylene. Machine stitch the frilling to the Terylene through the lace edging so that the frills are free (*diagram 1*).

Finishing Fit the frilled Terylene around the basket and pin the short ends. Machine stitch on the wrong side and catch the seam allowances down. Put the frilled cover back on the basket and stitch the top edge to the basket. Cut a piece of insert lace to fit round the top edge and insert pink and blue ribbons. Hem neatly around the top of the basket. Thread ribbons through a piece of insert lace to fit along the handle. Hand-sew to the handle along both edges. Make bows with the remaining ribbons and leave the ends about 10cm (4in) long. Sew the bows to each corner of the basket.

Basket from a seed tray

A gardener's seed tray made of plastic can be made into a baby basket for toiletries, using a pretty cotton fabric.

To cover the basket Cut a piece of Terylene wadding to fit the bottom of the tray. Cut a piece of the cotton fabric to fit inside the tray with about 12mm (½in) extra all round. Sew the fabric to the wadding with big stitches about 50mm (2in) apart.

Cut strips of fabric to the depth of the tray plus 25mm (1in) and three times the circumference. Join the strips and then join the short ends. Machine stitch both long edges to neaten. Gather the strip with long machine stitches, stitching two rows about 12mm (½in) from the top edge. Pull up the gathering to fit round the basket. Fold and stitch two strips of fabric, 90cm × 50mm (36in × 2in). Press the strips. Pass the strips under the tray and tie them on top. Put the frill on the tray and put in the lining. Pin and baste lining to frill, catching in the straps.

Remove the cover from the basket and machine stitch the frill to the lining on the wrong side. Put the cover back on the basket so that the straps are underneath, as shown in *diagram 2*.

Baby basket

Materials required

Fruit basket
Quilted fabric, cotton, nylon or plastic, 1m × 90cm (1yd × 36in)
Lining fabric, preferably white cotton 1m × 90cm (1yd × 36in)
Outer cover fabric, white Terylene or nylon, 30cm × 1m (12in × 36in)
Frilled nylon edging, 6m (6yd)
Nylon lace, 6m (6yd) 25mm (1in) wide
Insert lace, 1.5m (1½yd) 37mm (1½in) wide
Narrow blue and pink ribbons, 3m (3yd) each
Clear, all-purpose adhesive, cotton wool
Sewing threads

Tools you will need

Tape measure
Scissors
Needles, pins
Paper for pattern making
Sewing machine

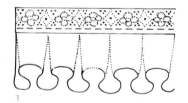

Daisy Mae rag doll

Rag dolls are always loved by their owners.
Every one made looks quite different from every
other rag doll and this doll is no exception. The
doll is approximately 60cm (24in) tall when
finished.

To make the doll

Making the pattern If you are using dressmaker's squared paper, copy the pattern pieces
from the graph. If you are using tracing paper,
draw an area 45cm (18in) square. Divide it into
25mm (1in) squares. Copy the pattern pieces for
the doll.

Cutting out Cut the paper pattern into pieces
and pin to the doubled fabric. Cut out the head
and body pattern. You will have two pieces. Cut
out the arm pattern once (2 pieces for one arm)
and then unpin the pattern and re-pin to the
doubled fabric for the second arm. Cut out the
leg shape (2 pieces for one leg) and then re-pin
the pattern and cut out the second leg (2 pieces).

Sewing the body Mark the arm placement dots
on the body pieces with basting thread marks.
Pin and baste two body pieces together, right
sides facing. Machine-stitch, using zigzag
stitch. Leave under-body and arm placements
open. Trim seams, turn right side out. Stuff
head and neck firmly, pushing stuffing in with
knitting needle.

☐ ARMS AND LEGS Sew 2 arm pieces together.
Clip between fingers and thumb. Trim seams.
Turn to right side. Stuff firmly. Make up second
arm. Make up two legs.

☐ JOINING ARMS AND LEGS Turn the seams in
at body armholes. Insert arms. Pin and then
hand-sew arms to body.

Finish stuffing the body. Insert the legs in the
under-body opening. Pin in position. Push in

any more stuffing that seems to be needed.
Oversew the body to the legs. (Make sure the
seams are down the front and back of the legs.)

Face and hair

☐ FACE Sew the button eyes in place. Mark and
then embroider the mouth with 2 strands of red
thread, using stem stitch. Embroider eyebrows
in 2 strands of black thread, using stem stitch.

☐ HAIR Cut 8 lengths of yarn 60cm (24in) long.
Keep these for ringlets.

Cut a piece of card about 12.5cm × 20cm (5in
× 8in). Wind the rest of the yarn round the
12.5cm (5in) depth of card 50 times. Thread a
short length into the needle and push through
the skein on the card. Slip the loops off, drop off
the needle and tie the yarn ends together.

☐ PUTTING THE HAIR ON Arrange the skein of
yarn so that loops lie along the seam on top of
the head and along the back of the neck. Stitch
the loops to the head. The skein should cover
the back of the head (*diagram 1*).

☐ MAKING RINGLETS Take 4 of the cut lengths.
Hold the ends in one hand and twist the strands
together until the wool turns. Put both ends of
twist together and pull to make little ringlets.
Stitch to the side of the head (*diagram 1*). Make
ringlets with the remaining 4 lengths of yarn.

☐ TOP HAIR Using the strip of card again, wind
the remaining yarn round the 20cm (8in) depth
of the card. Thread the skein on yarn as before
and tie the ends. Stitch the skein along the
middle to the top of the doll's head. Take the
loops to each side of the head (*diagram 2*).

Catch down above ringlets with stitches.

Making the doll's clothes

Making the pattern Draw up the 6 pattern
pieces for the dress, pinafore and pantaloons.

Dressing the doll

☐ DRESS Cut a piece of fabric 66cm × 23cm (26in
× 9in) for the dress skirt. Stitch lace to one long
edge. Cut out 2 sleeves, 1 dress bodice (front), 2
dress bodices (back). Stitch bodice backs to

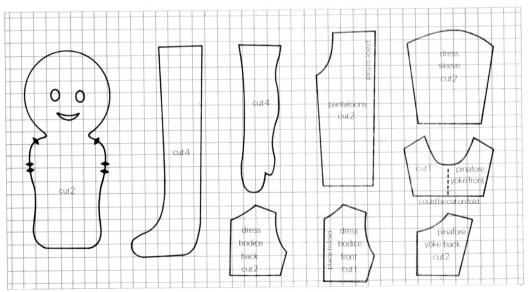

bodice front on side seams and shoulder seams. Neaten bodice back opening. Stitch lace to sleeves at wrist edges. Join under-arm seams. Stitch sleeves into bodice from wrong side. Join short sides of skirt for centre back seam, leaving 75mm (3in) open at waist. Neaten the opening. Gather waist edge and stitch to bodice. Sew buttons on dress back. Make cotton loops for fastenings.

□ NECK FRILL Cut a strip of fabric 250mm × 25mm (10in × 1in). Fold along length and press. Neaten short ends. Gather raw edges to fit dress neck. Pin, baste and stitch in place.

□ PINAFORE For the skirt, cut a strip of calico 23cm × 45cm (9in × 18in). Cut out 3 yoke pieces. Measure a 19cm (7½in) long panel in the centre of the skirt. Work 5 rows of gathering stitches from the top at 12mm (½in) intervals. Pull threads to make a 60mm (2½in) square block of gathering which can be smocked (diagram 3).

Join yoke pieces at shoulders. Neaten neck and armhole edges. Fold a hem on the yoke edge, top stitch onto the pinafore skirt. Neaten back openings. Sew on a button and make a thread loop to fasten the pinafore. Make a 37mm (1½in) square pocket. Sew it on the pinafore. Make a tiny handkerchief to match the dress.

□ PANTALOONS Cut out 2 pantaloon pieces. Sew lace on leg ends. Sew inside leg and crutch seams. Make casing at waist. Insert elastic to fit.

□ MOB CAP Cut a circle of calico 20cm (8in) diameter. Gather broderie Anglaise, pin and baste round the edge of the circle. Attach with zigzag stitch. 25mm (1in) in from the edge of the calico, work 2 rows of shirring elastic (diagram 4). Finish with a bow from scraps of dress fabric.

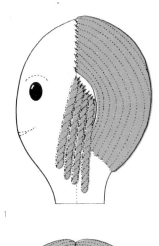

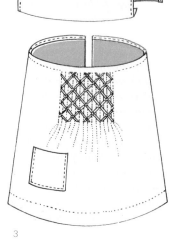

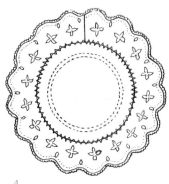

Embroidered apron

Apron

Materials required

Gingham fabric, ½ metre of 90cm wide (½yd of 36in wide) use fabric with 12mm (½in) squares
Bias binding, one card of 12mm (½in) wide

Embroidery threads, blue
Sewing thread to match the gingham and the contrast binding

Tools you will need

Tracing or greaseproof kitchen paper
Scissors

Pencil, ruler
Dressmaker's chalk pencil
Embroidery needle
Sewing needle
Sewing machine

This is just the kind of gift a godmother, grandmother or aunt could make for a little girl who likes to look pretty. The basic apron pattern can be adapted for all kinds of decorative sewing techniques. You can work the cross stitch decoration as illustrated or embroider small flowers in some of the gingham squares. Or you might stitch a pretty appliqué motif on the bib, or on the pockets. The apron could be made in a striped fabric with feather stitching and chain stitches worked between the coloured stripes. Or why not make up a piece of patchwork in squares to make the apron, backing it with a plain white fabric. A plain fabric apron could have flowerets of patchwork hexagons on the

pockets. You can use this pattern in so many ways, and with different kinds of fabrics. Plasticised cotton, for instance, in a bright colour, would make a useful washing up apron for a helpful daughter.

Making the pattern Mark out an area on the tracing paper 43cm × 20cm (17in × 8in). Mark it into 25mm (1in) squares. Copy the pattern line for line from the graph pattern into your squares. Mark in the pockets. This pattern is for half of the apron. The long, straight edge is the middle and you will be placing this on the fold of the fabric.

Cutting the fabric Fold the gingham lengthwise. Pin the paper pattern straight edge to the fold. Cut out. Mark the pockets' positions with basting thread. Cut a strip of gingham 40cm × 7cm (16in × 3in) for the halter neck. Cut two strips 45cm × 7cm (18in × 3in) for the waist ties. Cut two pocket pieces from the paper pattern.

Working the embroidery Cross stitch is one of the counted thread techniques and you do not need to mark the fabric. Cross stitch is especially easy when working on gingham. You simply embroider crosses in the gingham squares. To position the motif illustrated on an apron made with 6mm (¼in) squares, measure across the width of the bib and mark the centre with a pin. From the top edge count four gingham squares down and then count 14 more squares. Where the fourteenth square meets the line of the pin is the centre cross of the big flower motif. You can begin counting and working cross stitches from this point. The fabric illustrated has 6mm (¼in) squares. If the fabric you are using has squares of a smaller size, start the embroidery 106mm (4¼in) down from the top edge. You may have to make the flower stem longer. On 6mm (¼in) squared fabric, the motif is approximately 42cm (16½in) deep.

Making up the apron After the embroidery is completed, press the work on the wrong side. Stitch thread ends in neatly. Bind the edges of the pocket pieces with the bias binding. Machine stitch the pockets to the apron on three sides, leaving the top edge open. Bind the edges of the apron.

Making the straps and ties Fold the strips lengthwise, right sides facing and machine stitch along the short end, pivot at the corner and continue along the long side towards the middle of the strip. Stop stitching about 5cm (2in) from the middle. Cut the threads and then start stitching again, 5cm (2in) from the middle thus leaving a gap in the seam 10cm (4in) wide. Stitch to the corner, pivot and finish the other short end. Trim the seam allowances and trim the corners diagonally. Turn the strip to the right side. Press and then close the open seam with tiny oversewing stitches.

Make up the waist ties in the same way. Stitch the ties to the apron sides in the positions marked on the graph pattern. Stitch the halter to the neck edge. Press.

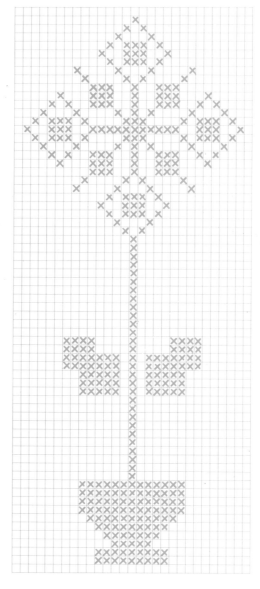

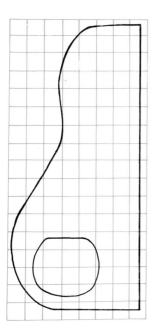

FAR LEFT: *Graph pattern for apron*
LEFT: *Embroidery stitch key*

21

Canvaswork pincushion

Canvaswork pincushion

Materials required

Clark's Anchor tapisserie wool in
  the following colours and
  quantities: 1 skein each Violet
  095, 099, Muscat Green 0281,
  Canary Yellow 0288, Amber
  Gold 0565.
Single thread canvas 23cm (9in)
  square, 14 holes to 25mm (1in)
Sewing thread to match velvet
Velvet fabric 30cm (12in) square
Small amount of Kapok or foam
  chip filling
Card for stiffening
Adhesive tape

Tools you will need

Tapestry needle No. 18
Scissors, tape measure
Sewing needles

Small, handworked accessories make a home
look charming and everyone appreciates a gift
that will enhance their home. Small pincushions, embroidered on canvas and trimmed with
velvet in a glowing colour make lovely gifts
whether they are intended for practical use or
simply for decoration. The pincushion illustrated is worked in satin stitch — a very quick
and easy canvaswork technique which anyone
can do — even if canvaswork has never been
tried before.

To work the embroidery Oversew the edges of
the canvas to prevent the edges from ravelling.
Mark the centre of the canvas with vertical and
horizontal basting stitches. Follow the illustration for the direction in which to work the
straight stitches. The diagram shows you how
many threads of canvas should be covered by
each stitch. The open arrow at the right shows
the centre of the design — one half of the design
only is shown. Begin embroidery at the point

marked by the small black arrow at the left of the
diagram. The diagram shows which colours you
should use.

Finishing the pincushion When all the
embroidery is completed, trim the canvas to
within 12mm (½in) of the embroidery. Cut a
piece of velvet to the shape of the embroidery.
This is for the pincushion base. Cut a strip of
velvet 64mm (2½in) deep to fit round the pincushion with 12mm (½in) overlaps. Sew the short
ends of the velvet strip together. Sew one edge
to the embroidered top from the wrong side,
working close to the stitches using back stitch.

Stiffen the sides by cutting a strip of card
45mm (1¾in) deep to fit round pincushion.
Overlap the ends 6mm (¼in) and join with tape.
Bend the card to the shape of the pincushion and
insert it inside the pincushion, against the velvet
strip. Sew the velvet base to two sides, turning
in the raw edges and using oversewing stitches.
Stuff the cushion firmly and complete the
sewing to close the seam. You might like to
finish the seam afterwards with neatly worked
Cretan stitch, using stranded embroidery cotton
in a colour to match the velvet or perhaps to
contrast with it.

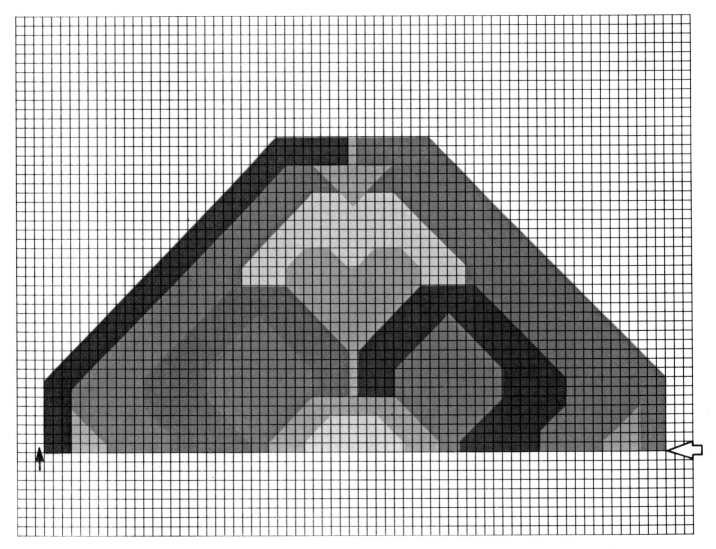

Handkerchief gifts

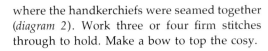

Coffeepot cosy

Materials required

3 handkerchiefs 30cm (12in), all the same pattern

Cotton fabric for lining 60cm × 90cm (24in × 36in)

Scrap of ribbon or bias binding for a bow

Terylene wadding, 30cm × 90cm (12in × 36in)

Sewing threads

Tools you will need

Pins, sewing needle
Scissors
Sewing machine

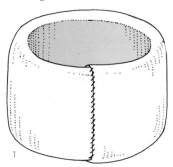

Handkerchiefs are useful gifts. Everyone needs them — everyone gets them. But you can make handkerchiefs into more exciting gifts with a little ingenuity and a little sewing. Here are some ideas for making quite inexpensive handkerchiefs into something very different.

Coffeepot cosy

Three handkerchiefs stitched together and sewn over a padded lining make a tea or coffeepot cosy. The handkerchiefs used in the illustration were 30cm (12in) square.

To make the cosy Fold each of the handkerchiefs in half, wrong sides facing. Iron the fold. Machine stitch along the fold on the right side, about 3mm (⅛in) from the edge.

Fold the cotton lengthwise, right sides together. Lay the wadding on the cotton and baste them together. Machine stitch, working from the cotton side, through all thicknesses, along one long side, along a short side and along the other long side. Leave the short end unstitched.

Trim the wadding back almost to the stitching line. Trim the cotton seam allowance to about half and cut off the corners diagonally. Turn the lining to the right side. Insert the stitched short end into the open short end. Turn a hem on both edges of the open seam and hem to make a padded lining ring (*diagram 1*).

Machine stitch the three handkerchiefs to make a ring, taking only 6mm (¼in) seams, and stitching on the wrong side. Press the seams open.

Slip the handkerchief ring over the padded ring. Oversew the top edges of both together. (If you prefer, work Cretan stitch or Feather stitch to join the cover and lining, using a matching, stranded embroidery thread.)

Draw the cosy together at the three points

where the handkerchiefs were seamed together (*diagram 2*). Work three or four firm stitches through to hold. Make a bow to top the cosy.

Fancy cushions

Men's large, white handkerchiefs make good-sized day bed cushions. Stitch four together along the hemline on three sides. Insert a cushion pad and close the fourth side by working small running stitches along the hemline. The hem stands out from the cushion. Cover two button moulds with cotton fabric, white, to match the handkerchiefs or a contrasting colour. Measure and mark the middle of the cushion on both sides with pins. Thread a needle with white button thread. Fasten the thread to one side of the cushion on the pin mark with a back stitch. Stitch on one button and then take the thread through the cushion to the other side and stitch on the second button. As you take the thread through the cushion, pull it fairly tight so that the cushion puffs up around the buttons.

Lacy pillow

You will need four lace-edged handkerchiefs and a piece of fine, cotton fabric for the cushion back. Using the zigzag stitch on the sewing machine, stitch the handkerchiefs together through the lace edges, to make a square. (If you are hand sewing, using tiny oversewing stitches.)

Cut the cotton backing to the same size as the joined handkerchiefs. Turn a hem on all four sides so that the square fits the fabric area of the seamed handkerchiefs, leaving the lace edges free. Machine stitch right on the edge, leaving one side open. Insert the cushion pad and close the seam with slip stitches. Make a rosette of narrow satin ribbon and sew to the middle of the cushion.

Hostess apron

You can make a pretty, long apron from 10 handkerchiefs sewn together, plus some matching ribbon for ties. Choose handkerchiefs in toning colours, or lace edged in a single colour or in a flower-sprigged pattern.

To make the apron Sew nine handkerchiefs together, three by three, to make a large square. Gather one edge of the square to the width of the tenth handkerchief, which will be the apron bib (*diagram 3*). Lay the handkerchief, right side down on the right side of the apron, edges matching and pin and baste. Machine stitch the gathered edge from the handkerchief (bib) side. Cut a piece of ribbon for the halter neck. Turn a narrow hem on the cut edges to the right side and pin and baste to the wrong side of the bib (*diagram 4*). Stitch, either by sewing machine or by hand using hemming stitches. Cut the remaining ribbon into two equal lengths. Turn a

LEFT: *Coffeepot cosy*

LEFT: *Lacy pillow (right) and
handkerchief cushion (behind)*
BELOW: *Hostess apron*

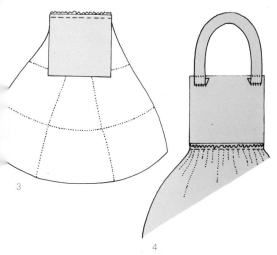

3

4

narrow hem to the right side on one end of both
pieces. Sew to each side of the apron at the
waist. Turn and sew a hem on both ends of the
ties to neaten.
Lace trimming For a pretty effect, add lace
trimming round the apron. Sew the lace to the
edges before sewing on the halter and waist ties.

More ideas

Children's handkerchiefs are often printed with
cartoon characters, animals, alphabet letters and
so on. Stitch 18 together, 3 across and 6 down.
Cut nylon wadding to fit and back it with cotton
to make a cot quilt cover. 9 large patterned
handkerchiefs will make a table cloth for a small
table. Two children's handkerchiefs will make
pretty nursery cushion covers, seamed
together. 8 handkerchiefs of the same colour or
of toning colours can be joined with faggoting to
make a long, pretty scarf.

Sewing box

Sewing box

Materials required

Two different fabrics ¼m (¼yd) of
  each
Light-weight cardboard
Clear, all-purpose adhesive
Sewing thread
Medium-weight Vilene ¼m (¼yd)

Tools you will need

Scissors
Pins, needles
Tape measure
Ruler, pencil

Making fabric boxes is quite an easy technique and in fact only the simplest sewing is required. The tricky part lies in measuring and cutting accurately. The pretty sewing box illustrated would make a delightful gift for a young girl but the same technique will make a jewel box or perhaps a box for notepaper, using a more luxurious fabric. Fabric boxes can be trimmed with ribbon, braid, lace edging or lurex braid, or the top can be decorated with embroidery, goldwork, beadwork or appliqué. All top decoration should be completed on the fabric before starting to cut out.

To start the box Fabric boxes consist of two layers of fabric covered card glued together. The lining piece is 3mm (⅛in) smaller all round than the outer piece. Decide first on the dimensions of the box you are making. The box illustrated measures 240mm × 126mm × 76mm (9½in × 5in × 3in) and has a hinged lid. Draw a plan of your box and 'explode' the pieces so that you can identify the four sides, the base and the top. Mark the dimensions clearly on each piece. This stage is very important.

Cut two pieces of card for each face (one smaller by 3mm (⅛in) all round). Mark each piece with a number so that you know which

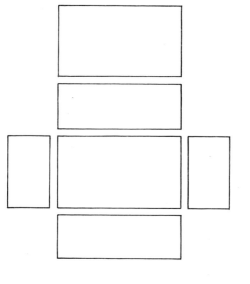

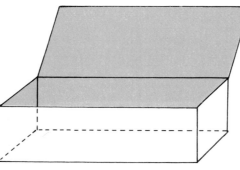

Sketch a box shape (right) and decide on the desired length, width and depth. 'Explode' the box shape (above), identify the pieces and mark the dimensions on each.

face of the box you are working with. The next stage is to cover all the pieces with Vilene.

Cut a piece of Vilene to the size of each piece of card exactly. Cut a second piece 9mm (⅜in) larger all round. Spread adhesive on the card and place it down on the larger piece of Vilene, folding the edges over onto the reverse side of the card and glueing them down. Glue the second piece of Vilene to the card to cover the raw edges. Identify the pieces again with pencil. Leave all the cards to dry under weights — books will do — protected by newspaper.

Outer layers Take the six outer pieces (the larger pieces). Cut out top fabric pieces to the size of the card plus 12mm (½in) all round. Spread adhesive round the edges of the card and fold the excess fabric over onto the adhesive. Fold the corners sharply and neatly. Press the turnings down firmly and then leave to dry under a weight. Prepare all six outer pieces in this way. Meanwhile, cover the lining cards in exactly the same way. When all six outer pieces and six lining pieces have been surfaced with fabric, they are glued together, but fastenings must be in position before this is done (see *Fastenings*). Spread adhesive thinly on the card side of a lining piece and on the card side of an outer piece. Take the adhesive up to the edges. When the adhesive has become tacky, press two surfaces together and leave to dry under weights. Complete all six sides of the box in the same way.

Constructing the box The box pieces are joined together with hand sewing, using either tiny oversewing stitches or Cretan stitch. Use a closely matching silk thread or three strands of embroidery thread. Work small firm stitches. Join the four sides first, and then attach the box base. Stitch the lid last.

Box divisions The sewing box illustrated has a dividing wall made of fabric-covered card; you might decide to sub-divide a jewel box into several compartments for rings and brooches etc.

To make a division, cut a single piece of card to exactly the measurements required and then cut two pieces of fabric to the same size plus 6mm (¼in) all round. Fold in 6mm (¼in) all round and press. Hold the two pieces of fabric together with the card sandwiched between and join with tiny oversewing stitches.

Round boxes are made in a very similar way to square or oblong ones. The side of a round or oval box is cut in one piece, the ends of the card butted and joined with Sellotape, afterwards covered with fabric.

Fastenings Fabric boxes are usually fastened with a loop and button. Insert a self-fabric loop fastening between the outer and inner box top before glueing them together. Stitch the button to the box front outer before glueing this to the box front inner.

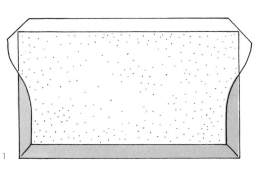

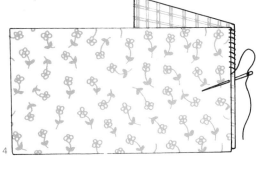

1 Mitre the corners of the Vilene and fold the edges over to the reverse side of the card.
2 Glue the second piece of Vilene to the reverse side of the card so that it is completely covered.
3 After positioning the fastenings, glue the lining pieces to the outer pieces, card sides together.
4 Join the sides of the box with hand sewing.

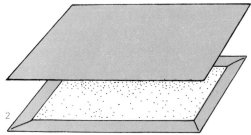

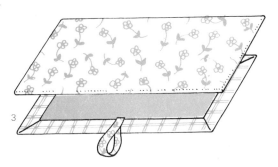

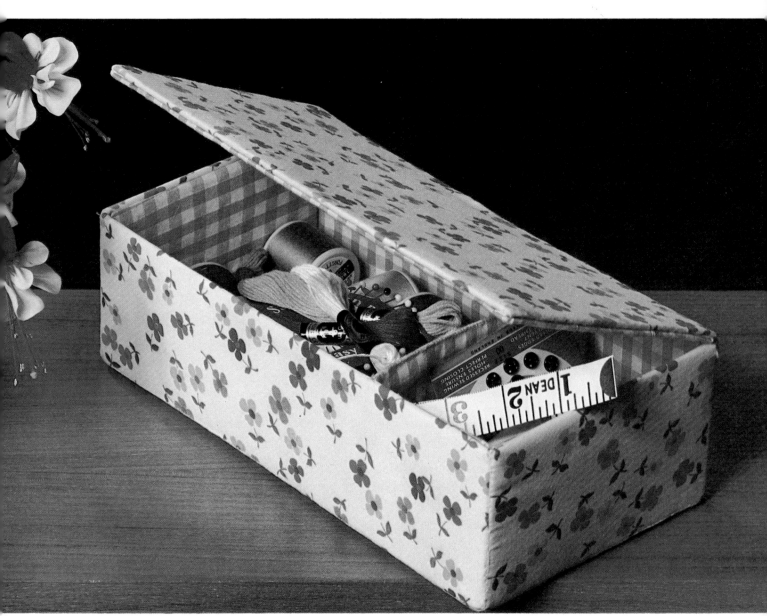

Flowers and herbs

Preserving flowers and herbs is an old craft and one that is within the reach of everyone. It does not matter whether you live in the country or in the town with just a window box for a garden, you can grow flowers and herbs for shape, colour and fragrance. Preserving plants is an all-year-round occupation. In the spring, you choose your young plants and seeds, gathering the blossoms and leaves in the summer and autumn. In winter, you spend relaxed and happy hours making pretty immortelles, sewing fragrant herb cushions and sachets or designing beautiful flower collage pictures.

Immortelles

Immortelles are arrangements of whole preserved flowers. If the flowers are picked at the right time and carefully preserved, quite a lot of the natural colour is retained. Preserved flower arrangements make lovely gifts and miniature flowers have a special appeal. The arrangement on the right is only 125mm (5in) high and uses a salt cellar as a container.

Flowers for miniature arrangements Many plants have small blossoms, others have heads of flowers which can be separated into flowerets. Some flowers — such as roses— have miniature strains. There is a vast selection to choose from and some can be grown in window boxes or even in flowerpots indoors. It is a good idea to obtain a seed catalogue and choose flowers for their colour, shape and size, and also for their foliage.

Drying methods Two methods of preserving can be used for whole flowers, air drying and drying with a desiccant. (A desiccant draws the moisture out of the plant. The most easily obtained and the most efficient desiccant is ordinary household borax powder.)

Flowers to air-dry

STATICE This has small flowers in different shades of blue. There are several species.
GOLDEN ROD Choose a species called *Solidago Lamore* for pretty cream-coloured flowers.
ACHILLEA Heads of flowers in clusters which can be separated

AFRICAN DAISY Golden, button-like flowers in clusters
HELICHRYSUM Popularly known as 'Everlastings'. They come in various colours and the flowers are preserved as buds before they open out
XERANTHEMUM Daisy-like flowers with silky petals, in pink, mauve, cream and white
PEARL EVERLASTING Clusters of white flowers
COTTON GRASS Small yellow flowers
HYDRANGEA Heads of florets which can be separated, pink or blue
MUGWORT Silvery-grey foliage
Some grasses can be preserved by air-drying methods and the following, some of which are wild, are attractive in miniature arrangements.
MAT GRASS Grey-green leaves and flower spikes
SILVER HAIR GRASS Tufts of silver flower heads
COMMON COUCH GRASS Blue-green stalks and flower spikes
QUAKING GRASS Tiny, pale green spiked heads on thin stalks
HARE'S TAIL Pale green tufted heads

Picking and preparing Gather flowers, leaves and grasses on a dry day and when the sun has been up for a while, so that any moisture has dried off. Choose flowers at the perfection stage of their growth, before they become too fully blown. Golden Rod is best cut when it is not quite in full bloom. Helichrysum flowers should be picked when the buds are open just enough to look attractive. Sort your plants into bunches, keeping the different kinds together. Tie the bunches with raffia or soft twine — or use soft sewing thread for plants with fragile stems. Roll the bunch lightly in tissue paper to prevent the colours from fading and tie the roll loosely. Hang the bunches with the heads downwards in a dry place where the light is not too strong. This could be an outhouse or even an upstairs room. Leave the bunches for two or three weeks or until the plants feel dry to the touch.

Drying in a desiccant Drying by this method enables you to preserve the whole flower head. You will need a large size carton of household borax and empty shallow cardboard boxes with lids. The type of box that contains a man's shirt is ideal. Spread a layer of borax about 25mm (1in) deep over the bottom of the box. Make

small indentations. Place a flower or floret in the indentation, making sure that petals do not touch, and then sprinkle borax over the flower gently. (A flour sifter is perfect for this). Cover the flowers completely and then put the lid on the box. Leave the box in a warm, dry place — such as an airing cupboard. The flowers will dry in quite a short time — from two to seven days. To see if the flowers are dry, lift one out and if the stem is stiff and the head feels firm, it is finished. To remove any powder clinging to the petals, hold the flower in one hand and tap the wrist with the other hand. If any still remains, blow the powder away. Store your preserved flowers in the same type of shirt box, lining the box with a piece of Terylene wadding to protect the flowers.

Flowers to dry in borax

MINIATURE ROSES There are different species in different colours. *Fairy* which produces pink flowers has perfect buds which are very suitable for miniature arrangements.

FORGET-ME-NOT Blue, pink and white flowers
CHRYSANTHEMUM PALLUDOSUM White, daisy-like flowers
CYNOGLOSSUM Sprays of sky-blue flowers
CLARKIA Pink, blue, mauve and white flowers
LARKSPUR Pink, blue, mauve and white flowers
PRIMULA Yellow flowers
GYPSOPHILA White and pale pink
POLYANTHUS Flowers of various colours
PANSIES Various colours
SYRINGA Lilac, mauve, white and cream
PHILADELPHUS Miniature mock orange, small white or cream flowers
ERICA HEATHER Tiny flowers in shades of purple
POLYGONUM Very small pink and white flowers

Many wild flowers can be preserved in borax which is a lovely way of keeping flowers which have so short a natural life. These flowers can be picked and preserved: flowers of the elderberry, may, clover, daisies, buttercups and primroses.

Stems for florets

Fine, florist's wire is used for making stems for flowers and florets. If the wire is inserted into the stem before the plant is dried, the stem dries around the wire, gripping it as it shrinks. The wire gives the stem additional strength.

Containers for miniature arrangements

Look around for small ornaments, glasses, tiny cups and bowls. Perfume bottles can be used, egg cups and small food jars. The caps from jars and bottles, painted gold or silver, look quite amazingly pretty. The base of wooden cotton reels, cut off and with a short length of dowelling glued to it makes a miniature pedestal. Glue a small bottle cap to the top of the dowelling. Fill containers with a piece of dry, florist's block, cut to fit tightly and push the flower stems into the block.

Pressed flowers

Pressed flowers are used for making collage pictures, for decorating book covers and box tops and for making very pretty and personal gift cards. For cards, book covers and book marks, the flowers are covered with self-adhesive transparent film to protect them.

Most flowers will press well but if they have thick fleshy centres, you should press the petals separately. Cut large heads of florets into separate flowers. Bell-like flowers, such as daffodils, snowdrops and lily-of-the-valley can be cut in half with scissors. Press some leaves too — ivy leaves keep their colours well. Choose silvery coloured leaves, such as Silver Carpet, for making Christmas greetings cards. They have a pretty, wintry effect on a dark paper and look like little firtrees. Ferns press well — cut individual fronds to make small sprays.

The secrets of successful pressing There is one most important secret to successful pressing and that is patience. Once the flowers are put away, they must not be disturbed for at least four weeks. If you peep to see how they are getting on, you will disturb them before the process has been completed. In four weeks, most flowers will have dried papery thin. Some leaves may take a little longer.

The longer plants are left pressing, the better the finished result will be. The drying-out process continues for several months and, if you can leave them, the colours are less likely to fade when the flowers are used to make a card or a picture.

Materials and equipment Flower presses can be purchased at some craft shops. You can make a simple flower press yourself or simply use a big, thick book and white blotting paper. You should supply yourself with a lidded tin box for collecting flowers for pressing. Line it with damp white blotting paper. You will also need a pair of scissors or clippers for cutting flowers and a pair of tweezers. Some labels for identifying your pressed flowers and some transparent envelopes for storing them and you have all the equipment you need. For the best results, collect flowers on a dry day, as soon as the dew has dried from the petals and leaves.

Pressing in a book Choose a book with a large page size and fairly thick. Start at the back. Lay a sheet of blotting paper on the right hand page. Lay a flower on the paper and with the tip of the tweezers, coax the stem into a curve. Several flowers and leaves can be arranged on the page but they must not touch or overlap. When the page is full, place another piece of white blotting paper on top. Be careful and work slowly because a sudden draught can cause everything

1

Gifts to make from dried flowers include a flower picture and finger plate for a door.

to drift about. Turn several pages of the book onto the blotting paper. Insert another sheet of blotting paper and begin the next arrangement. Continue in the same way until the book is full. Write yourself a note so that you know what is in the book and the date you prepared the pressing. Put the book away under a pile of books or with a kitchen weight on the cover, for at least four weeks. Do not disturb it for any reason.

Flower press

A flower press, complete with a supply of white blotting paper and some transparent envelopes or a photograph album with transparent film pockets would make a delightful gift for someone who loves flowers.

To make the flower press Drill a hole to fit the screws in the corners of both pieces of plywood (*diagram 1*). Cut the corners off all the pieces of corrugated cardboard so that they fit on the base (*diagram 2*). Cut the corners off the sheets of white blotting paper. Insert the screws into the bottom piece of plywood. Lay a piece of corrugated card on the plywood base. You are ready to use the flower press.

Filling the flower press Place a piece of blotting paper on the corrugated card. Arrange the flowers and place another piece of blotting paper on top. Lay the second piece of corrugated card on top of the blotting paper and then another blotting paper sheet. Arrange the next group of flowers and cover it with blotting paper as before. Continue making layers of blotting paper and flowers with corrugated card separating the layers until the press is full, finishing with a piece of corrugated card. Lay the second piece of plywood on top, fitting it onto the ends of the four screws. Put on the wing nuts and screw them down, a little on each screw in turn, until the press is closed.

Flower pictures

Pressed flower collage is a most creative craft and the most beautiful arrangements can be produced. You need not keep to pictures of flowers and leaves although these are lovely in themselves.

The background fabric can be woven material or a coloured, nonwoven fabric. Textured paper is also suitable. Use a latex adhesive, such as Copydex, because this can be removed easily without staining the background. Be careful of this type of adhesive on thick, textured fabrics. If you are working on tweed, for instance, it might be better to use a clear, all-purpose adhesive, very sparingly because the latex gets between the fibres and cannot be rubbed out. Do not use tweezers for arranging the pressed flowers. It may damage them. Use a soft paint brush. The bristles will lift the petals quite easily. Flower pictures should always be framed under glass to protect them. The glass must lie directly on the dried flowers so that there is no danger of condensation forming under the glass.

Other ideas for pressed flowers

Place individual pressed flowers in small transparent envelopes and slip them into letters or gift cards, or into a book.

Make calendars or notebook covers by covering a pressed flower arrangement with clear, adhesive film. Cover the tops of boxes with white or coloured paper and make a flower arrangement. Cover with adhesive film. Match-boxes make pretty gifts treated in this way with a miniature arrangement. Perspex door finger plates can be made to look very pretty with a flower arrangement on white card. Cut the card to the size of the finger plate, decorate with flowers and then cover with the perspex plate. A set of flower plates would make a delightful gift for a housewarming.

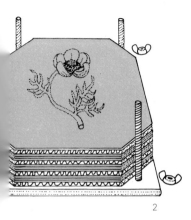

Flower press

Materials required

Two 30cm (12in) squares of bonded plywood

Four long screws 10-15cm (4-6in) long. (If the screws have heads, you will need only 4 wing nuts for the other end. If the screws are headless, you will need 4 nuts as well as wing nuts).

6 sheets of corrugated card, 30cm (12in) square

White blotting paper

Tools you will need

Drill, sharp crafts knife

Sweet-smelling gifts from flowers and herbs

There is nothing so charming, nor as memorable as a gift of fragrant dried flowers and herbs, made up into a sachet or presented in a pretty container. Dried flower and herb mixtures can be purchased fairly inexpensively, so that you can make up the sachets with ready-blended fragrances. Alternatively, grow your own flowers and herbs and mix your own pot-pourris at home, adding essential oils and spices to your own tastes.

Choosing flowers and leaves The best way to choose your scented flowers is to go round the garden and sniff. There are so many sweet-smelling flowers which you can use. Here are just a few: roses, lavender, geraniums, jasmine, wallflowers and orange blossom. Hyacinths, violets, jonquils, narcissus, lilac and honey-suckle. Gardenias, lily of the valley and syringa. Rose geranium leaves, eucalyptus, cornflowers, nasturtiums, cowslips, marigolds, borage and camomile add a touch of astringency to mixtures.

Of the herbs which you can grow, lemon balm, lemon verbena, thyme, all the mint varieties, lovage, marjoram, sage, tarragon, and rosemary, all have distinctive fragrances for mixtures.

Spices and other ingredients Some of the spices can be used in pot-pourris — ground cloves, nutmeg, cinnamon, mace, vanilla in pod form and woodruff. Dried hops are good for making sleep pillows for restful sleep. Essential oils, which can be bought from herbalist shops and some chemists, are used in minute quantities of a few drops. Oil of rose, oil of sandalwood and oil of citrus are the ones most used in preserving flowers and herbs. Dried orange and lemon peel, cut into thin strips or pieces can be added to mixtures.

Harvesting flowers and herbs Flowers should be picked when they are at their most perfect, early in the day and as soon as the dew has dried from the petals. Herbs are at their best just before they flower in the early autumn. Small flowers can be left whole. Larger flowers can be pulled apart and just the petals used.

Drying methods In ideal conditions, the plants should dry without going mouldy, should keep some of their colour and all of their scent. Too much heat and light will drive off the perfume and turn the blossoms brown. If the air is moist, the plants will not give up their own moisture and will rot. The ideal is a dark place, with a little warmth and some air. This might be an airing cupboard or a cupboard or attic room where you can use a small heater. A cellar or a basement where there is a boiler will do, if there is very little daylight. The best kind of tray for drying flowers and herbs is an old frame with a piece of muslin tacked across it. Ordinary shallow cardboard boxes will do if the bottom is pierced with holes. Do not use a wire cake tray or metal mesh of any kind. After collecting the flowers and leaves, leave them on their stems and arrange them on your tray. Pick only sufficient to fill the trays you have available. Do not pile the trays. The flowers can touch one another but do not try to fill every available space. Lay the tray on a shelf, resting on pieces of wood so that the air can circulate round the tray.

Conditions and temperatures will vary so it is impossible to say exactly how long it will take for your flowers to dry. It could be anything from five to fifteen days. The plants will feel dry and slightly crisp but they should not be so dry that they break into bits when you handle them. If, while the drying is going on, the store place seems full of perfume, then there is too much heat and you are driving off the scent. Move the trays to a cooler place. Turn the flowers and leaves over with your fingers while they are drying.

Use dried plants immediately or store them in airtight tins or jars until you are ready to use them.

Airdrying herbs Stems of lavender and herbs are best dried by hanging in a warm place where there is dry air. Pick the plants just before they flower. Lavender should be only just out of the bud stage for the fullest perfume. Tie the plants in small bunches and hang them, heads down, in a dark place so that the colour is retained. Herbs can also be dried on trays in a just-warm oven but for the best flavour in cooking, the air-dry method should be used.

Pot-pourri

Pot-pourri can be a mixture of flowers, leaves, spices and oils. Experiment with mixtures until you have evolved your own special recipe. Keep note of the ingredients as you add them. You will need a main fragrance — this could be rose or lavender or hyacinths for instance. Add small quantities of other flowers and herbs but keep them to just four or five or the individual scents will be blanketed. Add a tablespoon or so of

A selection of ideas for sweet-smelling gifts

powdered orris root to 'fix' the perfumes and make them last longer.

To make a pot-pourri Choose an attractive container. This can be a china jar or a silver bowl, a pretty dish or a large shell. Make the pot-pourri in a large jar with a screw-on lid. Choose your flowers and herbs and dry them. Add essential oils and spices, and the fixative powder. Put the dried plants in layers in the jar, screw on the cap and leave for about 6 weeks.

When the mixture has blended thoroughly, spoon it into your container. Add a few dried flowers to the top for extra colour. For a gift, cover the container with cling film wrap.

To make rose pot-pourri Gather rose petals, lavender spikes, lemon verbena leaves and geranium petals. Dry the petals and leaves slowly (see *Drying methods*).

Turn the petals each day but do not heap fresh petals on those already drying.

To approximately 2 quarts of petals, add the following mixture:

2oz each of ground cinnamon, ground cloves and allspice

4oz of powdered orris root

15 drops of rose oil and 5 drops of citrus oil.

Mix everything together and leave in an airtight container for about 6 weeks before using.

Flower sachets

Sachets can be any size, small enough to put into letters or in a box of notepaper — or large enough to use as a sleep pillow, resting near the sleeper's head. They can be given small hangers so that they can be used in cupboards or on coat hangers. They can take the form of small, pretty drawstring bags so that the contents can be renewed.

The sachets are usually made up of an inner and an outer bag. The inner bag, which holds the dried flowers or herbs, is made of fine muslin or organdie which allow maximum filtration of the perfume.

The outer sachet should be a thin, pretty fabric — lawn, silk, lace, dotted swiss, net or thin cotton. Trim sachets with scraps of ribbon, insertion lace, lace edging, silk flowers, velvet ribbons — anything which makes the sachet look delicate and feminine. If the sachet is to be embroidered with decoration or with a message, work the embroidery before making up the sachet.

To make a sachet Cut two pieces of muslin, for the inner bag, to the same size and shape. Join the two pieces together with machine stitching or hand-sewn back stitches, around three sides and part of the fourth. Turn to the right side. Fill with the chosen dried flowers and/or herbs and close the opening with oversewing stitches.

Cut your chosen fabric for the outer bag to the same size as the inner bag, plus seam allowances. Stitch around three sides and turn to the right side. Put the inner bag inside, turn in the seam allowances on the opening and join the seam with tiny oversewing stitches.

Lavender bag Make and fill the inner sachet first. Cut two pieces of fabric for the outer bag to the same size plus 9mm (³⁄₈in) extra on the depth. Place two pieces together and machine stitch on three sides. Turn a hem on the top edge and machine stitch first on the folded edge and then again 6mm (¼in) away.

Cut a tiny hole in this casing and buttonhole stitch the cut edges to neaten. Thread narrow ribbon through on a bodkin. Insert the muslin bag and draw up the bag top, hanging it from the ribbon loop.

Ribbon sachets Buy short lengths of beautiful ribbon, about 50mm (2in) wide. Fold it across and handsew the long sides together. Fill with dried mixture and hand sew the open end, slipping in a small ribbon loop.

Use ribbon to make a scented hairband. Make a muslin or organdie bag, 25mm (1in) wide and about 15cm (6in) long. Fill with dried mixture. Close the end. Cover the bag with a piece of pretty ribbon. Sew elastic to the ribbon ends.

Ideas for special gifts

Lavender fan

You will need 10 stems of lavender. Cut them to about 20cm (8in) long. Lay them on a flat surface and tie just under the heads. Cut a circle of stiff organdie, using a saucer as a pattern. Cut the circle in half. Trim with lace and ribbons. Sandwich the tied heads of lavender between the half-circles. Hand sew all round, stitching the stems in securely. Tie a satin ribbon bow to the stems. (A lavender fan is very refreshing to use on a hot evening!)

Moth bags

Mix rosemary leaves, tansy, thyme, mint and a very small amount of ground cloves. Blend carefully. Cut circles of thin patterned fabric with pinking shears, about 75mm (3in) across. Use two circles together. Put a spoonful of the mixture on the fabric and tie up with narrow ribbon. Put moth bags in drawers where you will keep jumpers and sweaters and hang them with a loop from coat hangers.

Pomander ball

Oranges are usually used for making pomanders but lemons and limes can also be used. Choose perfect unblemished fruit. Stud the fruit all over with cloves — a medium sized orange takes about 2oz of cloves. If the pomander is going to be hung, leave a strip about 6mm (¼in) wide all round the orange, so that a ribbon can be tied round the finished pomander.

Prepare a mixture of orris root powder and ½ teaspoons of cinnamon, allspice and cardamom powder. Add a drop or two of sandalwood oil if you have it — but it is not essential. Roll the orange in the powder and then wrap it in tissue paper with some of the powder. Put the orange away in a dark, cool place, such as a bureau drawer. The orange should dry hard and shrink, in about 2-3 weeks.

Perfume pots

Make these for a party table and tell the guests that they can take their perfume pot away with them after the party. You will need small glass pots or short stemmed wineglasses. Put in some fragrant flower and herb mixture, to within 12mm (½in) of the brim. Insert two or three whole dried flowers. Make a small ribbon bow, leaving the ends long. Spear the bow into the mixture with a loop of florist's wire. (Perfume pots were prepared in Elizabethan times for the royal banquets — not just for pretty table decoration but to mask any smells which might have offended the guests!)

Cook's gift

Choose four or five cotton gingham fabrics in different colours. Wash in hot water to remove any dressing and iron. Cut fabrics into 10cm (4in) circles with pinking shears. Make a herb mixture for bouquet garni — marjoram, thyme, parsley, sage and bayleaf. Put a large spoonful of the herbs on each circle. Tie up tightly with white cotton tape. Fill a large glass jar with bouquet garni balls.

Paint jobs

Painted tinware

Materials required

Old tin or enamelled objects,
 plates, mugs, water cans, jugs
 etc.
Undercoat paint
Gloss paint, dark green or black
Small tins gloss enamel, scarlet,
 yellow, white, black, green.
White spirit
White chalk

Tools you will need

25mm (1in) paint brush
Good quality soft-bristle artist's
 brush, round head, size 6.
Fine sandpaper if needed

Roses all the way

The bargee families, who used to live and work on Britain's canals and waterways, had an eye for colour and a love of flowers. Their life, constantly on the move, meant that they could never have gardens but instead they grew flowers in anything that would hold soil and carried their pot gardens along with them.

The barges themselves reflected the same love of colour. Every part of the barge that could be painted was decorated with geometric shapes, garlands of flowers or fabulous landscapes. The bargee artists were untrained in painting or drawing and so their flower decorations were done freely, the form of the brush itself making the rose petals and leaf shapes.

The designs illustrated are worked in this way and, even if you cannot draw, you will probably find that you can do barge flowers. Do not approach the job nervously. It is meant to be fun. If a leaf or petal goes wrong, wipe it off with a scrap of rag dipped in white spirit — and try again. Barge painted tinware makes lovely gifts — if you can bear to give them away, but remember, painted tinware cannot be used — it is for decoration only.

Preparing the tinware If the tinware is rusty, sandpaper the surface smooth. Rub down chipped edges. First, cover with undercoat and leave to dry. Paint all over the tinware with the dark green gloss paint. Paint the outside first, leave to dry, then the inside. Paint the bottoms of utensils too. When everything is completely dry, chalk out the design.

The motifs Five motifs are shown in *diagrams 1-4:* the full-blown rose (*1*), a bud (*2*), a daisy and leaves (*3*) and a garland (*4*). You could copy these or follow the motifs in the photograph. But do not necessarily follow the illustrated examples. Try painting a band of scarlet round a

plate, edging it with yellow. Paint garlands round the neck of a jug with a deep band of red round the bottom. Splash the colour around. The more colourful you make your tinware, the more like the traditional bargeware it will look.

Painting techniques Always let one colour dry before painting another on top. Enamel paints generally take about 12 hours to dry thoroughly.

□ ROSES Paint a circle first, about 60mm (2½in) across. A red rose goes on a black circle, a yellow rose on a red circle, a white rose on a yellow circle.

Try to paint each of the petals in two strokes only. Start with the pointed end; increase the pressure as you get to the wider end, and then lift the brush off, away from you. Dip the brush in the paint again, go back to the point and finish the petal, lifting the brush off towards you, as illustrated in *diagram 5*.

This method of increasing the pressure you put on the brush to widen a line, then lifting the brush gently to narrow it, is the basis of all the rose petals. You can paint the leaf shapes in the same way, painting half of a leaf at a time. Paint the leaf veins in yellow when the green is dry.

□ BANDS It will be difficult to get bands absolutely straight but chalk the line first and then clean the edge of the line afterwards with your fingertip covered in a scrap of rag dampened with white spirit.

Enamel paints are durable and do not chip easily but for extra protection, give tinware a coat of clear, polyurethane varnish when the paint is dry.

Decorating with paints

Decorating with paint can turn ordinary, unfinished household articles and accessories into attractive-looking gifts. The choice of wooden articles which can be painted is enormous. Craft shops usually have a range of boxes, shelves, cupboards, frames, napkin rings, candlesticks and so on. Second hand furniture shops will yield all kinds of old, varnished bric-à-brac which will look pretty and modern when they have been stripped, painted and decorated.

Which paints to use

Modeller's enamel paints are sold in tiny tins, comparatively inexpensively and the range of colours is wide. These colours can be intermixed quite easily and brushes are cleaned with white spirit.

Artist's acrylic polymer colours can be bought in tubes or in jars and these are water-based. They dry very quickly and brushes are cleaned in water immediately after using them. Both of these types of paint are hardwearing and have a glossy finish (although the acrylic colours are less glossy than enamels).

Beginners find poster colours easiest to use. They mix with water, go onto a surface smoothly, enable you to blend colours together and give a good coverage of an area, if that is required. To make poster colours durable, the painted piece can be given a coat or two of clear, polyurethane varnish after drying. Choose varnishes with care because some have a yellow tinge. Varnish sold in craft shops for decoupage is the best and is quite colourless.

Patterns and designs

If you have a certain amount of skill in drawing, you will find great pleasure in painting on wood. You can work directly onto a raw wood surface, using the wood colour as part of your design, or you can give the piece a smooth coat of white undercoat first. Designs can then be pencilled on the surface, and rubbed out with an eraser if necessary.

With a pair of compasses and a ruler, you can make lots of attractive geometric designs which can be transferred to boxes or other items. Overleaf there are ideas for different designs. Draw the design on ordinary tracing paper or greaseproof paper, pencil the wrong side all over and then tape the tracing to the surface to be decorated. Draw over the lines with a hard pencil and you are ready to start painting. Use just three or four colours and keep your design tracing to refer to, just in case you overpaint a line and lose the pattern. Once the paint is dry, you can always replace the tracing over the top and redraw lines you have lost.

Waterproof felt-tipped pens can be used for outlining shapes, if the item is going to be varnished afterwards.

Transfers There is no reason why you should not combine transfers and handpainting in your design. Transfers come in all sizes and in a wide variety of styles and pictures to suit all tastes. By mounting a flower transfer for instance, and then adding a garland of leaves or ribbons, you have produced an original design which perhaps looks better than if you have attempted to paint an intricate flower yourself.

Overpainting on gloss paint If a wood item has been painted with gloss paint, you will find it difficult to trace down using pencil. Ordinary chalk rubbed over the back of the tracing will make clear marks on the shiny surface, and can be rubbed away after the painting is finished.

Using masking tape Masking tape will help you to make designs based on lines, such as diagonal stripes. Paint the base colour first. Lay the tape across as you wish, and paint between the bands of tape. Leave to dry and gently pull off the tape.

Candle wax techniques Children enjoy this kind of technique and usually produce very interesting results, once they get the idea. Paint a wood surface, such as the lid of a trinket box, with white undercoat. Paint a design in poster colours and leave to dry. With a metal pen nib in a holder, scratch away lines on the design, so that the white shows through. You can scratch away quite big areas of paint if you like. Rub over the whole surface with an end of wax candle. With a finger nail, scratch out some of the white areas. Go over these areas with indian ink, using a pen or a brush. Polish the surface with a cloth.

You can also have fun with wax by dripping spots. Paint the item with a light-coloured undercoat or water-based paint. Drip wax onto the surface from a lighted candle. Let it splash. Brush another thin coat of colour over the surface. Let it dry and then splash on more

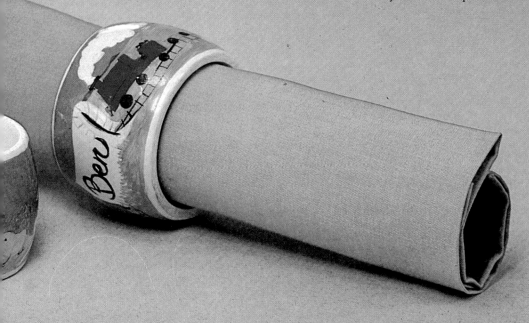

melted wax. Paint again. Scrape off the wax areas with a finger nail or a blunt knife tip.

Getting a good gloss finish Getting a really good gloss finish takes time and preparation. If the box or item you are preparing to paint has been painted before or if it has varnish on it, strip the paint off with a commercial stripper and then sandpaper the surface until it is smooth. Wrap a piece of coarse sandpaper round a block of wood and work in smooth straight strokes. Do not go round in circles because the wood could be permanently marked. Go on to use a finer sandpaper and sand until the surface feels satiny to the touch. If you like, you can fill old dents and holes with wood filler at this stage and then sand the surface smooth again.

Prime the wood with a primer. It seems a lot of trouble but it is worth it for a really good finish. Next, give the piece two thin undercoats, chosen to suit the colour of the final gloss paint. Sand down the surface again if bits of paint have dried and are spoiling the surface. When you are going to apply the gloss, choose a fairly warm day. Do not wear anything woolly. Close the windows if there is a breeze.

Check the paint brush to make sure that there are no loose hairs or flakes of paint left over from a previous painting job. Stir the paint carefully. Dip the bristles of the brush into the paint from above the middle of the pot, so that about half of the bristles pick up paint. Gently draw the bristles against the side of the tin to remove drips. Apply the paint lightly and immediately begin to brush out. This means spreading the paint in all directions from the place you applied it. It is quite hard work but if you persevere, you will be surprised how far you can spread one brushful of paint. Cover the area to be painted in exactly the same way. Aim for a thin coat of paint, well spread. Finally, brush all over the area with even strokes going in one direction, lifting the brush into the air at the end of a stroke. You will see that in a few minutes, the whole surface has smoothed itself out. The brushstrokes have gone and a high gloss, smooth surface remains. If you can immediately get the piece into a cardboard box lying on its side or under a 'tent' made of a piece of plastic sheeting, you will prevent dust from settling on the wet paint. Your finished result will be something to be proud of.

Here is a wide selection of motifs which you can trace off and use for decorating a variety of handicraft gifts.

Decorating with stencils

Stencils are one of the easiest ways of decorating with paint, if you cannot draw. A stencil is a design cut out of stiff, coated paper and paint is 'dabbed' onto the surface underneath the stencil, thus making a print of the cut-out design.

Ready-cut stencils of letters, flowers, animals, birds, houses and trees and so on can be bought quite easily from art shops and some stationers. The way in which you use the stencils to make decorative patterns is entirely up to you. Later, when you are more experienced in the craft, you will want to cut your own stencils and widen the scope of your designs.

Paints for stencilling

Water-based paints Beginners will find water-based paints easiest to use. Poster paints, used directly from the pot and rather thick, are simple to use and dry quickly. Two or three coats of clear polyurethane varnish will make the design hardwearing. Water colours are only suitable for stencilling designs on paper. Acrylic polymer paints are very good for most surfaces and large areas of design can be applied using a piece of close-textured synthetic sponge.

Oil paints These can be used for painting on china or gloss-painted surfaces but are not very suitable for untreated wood as the oil is likely to seep out of the colour, making a kind of 'halo' round the stencilled outlines. Modeller's enamels can be used for working small areas of design but they are rather thin in consistency and are likely to flood under the edges of the stencil unless care is taken. Spray enamels are useful for stencilling big projects. The spray paint dries very quickly and several coats can be applied, one after another. Spray enamels are good for stencilling on glass or china.

Fabric paints work well with stencilling techniques and are ideal for working designs on clothes, accessories and furnishings.

The basic technique of stencilling Place the stencil over the area to be painted. Tear or cut off small pieces of masking tape and position the tape on the edges of the stencil so that it is held firmly on the surface. Fill the brush with thick paint, and dab gently over the edges of the stencil, working towards the centre of the area. Do not apply too much paint or it will flood under the edge of the stencil. Adequate coverage of the area is all that is required. Leave the stencil in position for a few minutes, then carefully pull away the holding tape and lift the stencil. Wipe the stencil clean, paying particular attention to any smears on the underside. Let one colour dry before attempting to put another colour area down nearby. If you are lining up designs, such as when stencilling a border or putting letters in a line, draw a pencilled line right across the stencil under the cutouts and then pencil a line on the surface. You can then match up the pencilled lines. If you are stencilling on a transparent or shiny surface, such as glass, lay a piece of the masking tape across the glass and line the stencil up with the edge of the tape.

When a lettering stencil is being used on the inside or the outside of the glass, it may be useful to use double-sided masking tape. A curved surface makes it difficult to hold the stencil absolutely flat. Pieces of double-sided tape on the stencil itself will hold it firmly on a convex or concave surface.

Cutting your own stencils Stencil paper can be bought at most art shops. It is thick, brown and has a shiny surface. Designs can be drawn on the paper or, you can trace off outlines from books or from gift wrap and transfer them down onto the stencil paper. To cut stencils, a really sharp crafts' knife is needed. Use a metal ruler for cutting straight edges. When cutting curved lines, keep the fingers of the other hand well away from the blade. Hold the blade upright — do not lean it to the right or to the left — and draw the blade slowly towards you. Do not try to cut right through the stencil paper the first time. Rather, make several light cuts and keep a clean line.

Keep your designs simple because intricate patterns are difficult to cut out. When you are planning a shape, remember to leave bridges or 'stays'. These hold areas of the design to the outside border as shown in *diagram 1*. If you are cutting out a single shape, keep the piece that you cut out because you may be able to use it as a relief stencil and thus have two different effects that you can use as in *diagram 2*.

Gift ideas for using stencils

Make a fabric tote bag and stencil the owner's initials on it. Make a denim notebook cover and stencil motifs, perhaps related to a subject being studied. Stencil on T-shirts, hats, canvas shoes. Buy a canvas shoulder bag and make it special with stencilled flowers or a single motif. Stencil on a paper lampshade, on brown paper to make your own gift wrap, on plain notepaper to make it personalized. Paint wooden boxes and stencil designs to make them pretty for jewel boxes. Paint glass bottles and add stencilled designs for ornaments. Buy glass containers — or empty sweet jars. Stencil letters to make them into dry food storage jars for a kitchen gift. Do a set for use as spice jars, for instance.

Equipment you will need

Masking tape This can be obtained quite easily at art shops. It is a reel of sticky backed tape with a low-tack adhesive so that it can be pulled of surfaces easily and without damaging them. Artists and designers use it for masking out areas before painting murals or when spray-painting. In stencil work, it is used for holding the stencil in position while you apply paint. Two-sided tape is used when working on curved glass surfaces.

Brushes Only one kind of brush is used for stencilling. This is round, with a flat head. Have two, one for light colours and one for dark colours.

1

2

Pictures on stones

Painting pictures and designs on stones and pebbles may seem a new handicraft but, in fact, people have been doing it for thousands of years. Think of the cave paintings, where primitive artists have illustrated the wild animals they saw around them. The art in decorating stones lies in seeing the shape and texture and allowing these to suggest a design. Hold the stone in your hand, turn it and study the dents and imperfections. Balance it so that it stands firmly and look at the shape. Perhaps it suggests a cat sitting with its tail curled round its feet, or a squat bird, or perhaps a fish. Perfectly round, flattish pebbles may look like beetles, or eggs. Flat stones might take a design in geometric patterns or stripes.

The best place to find stones and pebbles of a workable size is on the beach, although some river beds have suitable stones. Garden stones have a rough surface usually, but stones from beach or mud banks are water-smoothed and are ready to use.

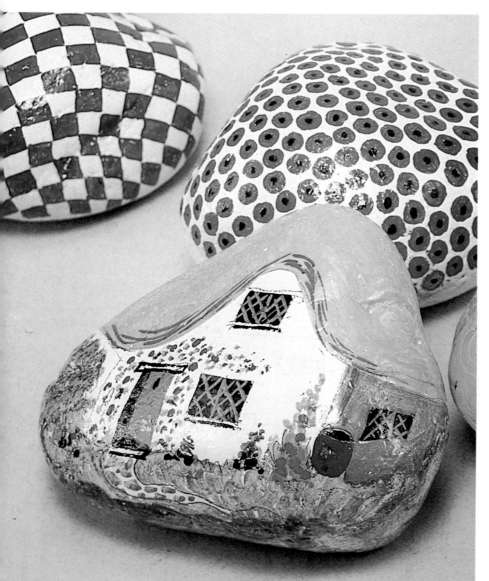

Clean the stones first. Wash them with hot water and a little liquid detergent and scrub off sand and mud. Rinse and leave them to dry out standing on a cotton reel or a glass jar. The stones must be dry before you can attempt to paint them and this could take some days with some types of stone.

Paints for stones Both oil and acrylic colours are used for stone and pebble painting, but the best medium for a beginner is water colour or poster paint. The advantage of these is that you can wash mistakes out easily and start again. Water colour paints should be used fairly thickly.

A set of poster colours, six jars, yellow, red, green, blue, black and white, will provide you with all the colours you need to begin with. With these you can mix most shades. Later you can add other colours to your original set.

Modeller's enamel paints, sold in small 25mm (1in) high tins are ideal for stone painting. The colour range is wide and there are some colours in metallic finishes which can be used for special effects. Modeller's enamels are oil-based and you will need some white spirit to clean your hands and brushes.

Paint brushes As with all painting hobbies and crafts, buy the very best brushes you can get. Sable brushes are best to use and if you look after them, they will last for months. When you are choosing a brush, look around and see if the shop has provided a small jar of water — many do. Dip the brush in the water and draw the point across the back of your hand. The point should be perfect when you hold the brush against the light. If odd hairs stand out from the sides or there appears to be a double point, reject that brush and try another. Brush sizes are very much a personal thing but you will probably find that a size 5 and a size 3 will be sufficient at the start. If brushes are used for oil paints, clean them thoroughly in white spirit between each colour and again at the end of the session. Wash out the spirit with hot water and detergent. Rinse in clean water and shake out the moisture. Stand in a jar, head up. Never leave brushes standing in water. The bristles will bend and you will never get them to straighten out again satisfactorily.

Undercoating Some stone artists like to paint the pebble with undercoat first so that they work on a smooth, one-colour surface. If you are painting an animal or a bird, you may be able to use the natural stone colour as part of the creature's fur or feathers. It is worth studying the colour variations of a stone before finally deciding to blank out the surface with undercoating. For undercoating, use a water-based emulsion paint. Paint one surface first and leave to dry balanced on a bottle or jar. Turn the stone over and finish undercoating.

Designing on a stone The first thing to remember about pebble painting is that it is meant to be fun. Finished stones make wonderful gifts. People use them as paper weights, table ornaments, for keepsakes and large ones make good doorstops.

□ PAINTS The design you decide on should be free and painted with a certain verve. If you feel that you cannot draw and could not possibly get the effect of animals, such as the charming rabbits illustrated, then try shapes that you *can* manage — spots, stripes, crosses like stars. There is no reason why you should not trace pictures from books or motifs from wallpaper. Rub soft pencil on the back of the tracing and impress your design down with a pencil. You might try a stencilled design or perhaps spray painting over a stone with some areas masked out with sticky tape. Even children can draw a house shape, with a simple rectangle for a door, and squares for windows. An oblong stone might be turned into a little house with a blue door, white-curtained windows and a red roof. Have fun by painting blobs of colour round the house for a flower garden.

Very small stones, painted with scenes and seascapes take skill and patience, but only you can assess how much you can attempt. The important thing is that you enjoy finding the right kinds of stones and feel inspired by something in the shape and colour.

□ TRANSFERS If you really do feel that painting of any kind is quite beyond you, why not decorate stones with decal motifs or transfers.

There is a wide variety of shapes and motifs in most craft shops, animals, flowers, fruits etc. Paint the stone in a single strong colour and apply the motif. Nothing could be simpler — or quicker! Rub-down letters, which can be bought from most stationers could be used to make words such as 'Urgent' or 'Bills to be paid' or with a loving message for remembrance.

Finishing stones Oil paints need no finishing but water-based paints should be given a coat of clear varnish. Choose varnishes carefully because some have a yellow tinge which spoils white and pale colours. Polyurethane varnishes dry hard and clear in just a few hours. Stand the stone on the neck of a jar or bottle and paint the varnish over the surface thinly. Allow to dry and then turn the stone over and paint the other side. When the first coat has dried, give the stone another thin coat.

If stones are being used for table decorations or paper weights, it is a good idea to glue a small circle of felt on the underside to protect polished surfaces.

Fabric painting

Children love animal cushions for gifts. The cushions can lie on beds during the day but at night, they become cuddly toys.

The easiest — and cheapest — way to make bright cuddle cushions is to paint them yourself on ordinary sheeting, using fabric paints. Cut up partially worn sheets or pillow cases and, to complete your re-cycling, stuff the cushions with boiled, chopped-up tights and stockings for a lightweight, washable filling.

Fabric paints have come a long way in the past few years and they are now as easy to use as poster colours. The colours are bright and intermixable and you paint them on straight from the bottle.

Owl cushion

Preparing the pattern Use a soft pencil for drawing on the sheeting, or chalk if you prefer. Spread the sheeting and draw a square shape for the owl's body. The square can be any size — the owls illustrated are about 30cm (12in) square. Draw a design on the body shape and round off the corners of the square. Draw out two ears and two feet shapes, working from the pattern opposite. The diagram is to a scale of 1 square to 40mm (1½in). On another part of the sheeting, draw another square for the back of the owl's body. Round off the corners as before and then pencil in the completion of your body design.

Put a wad of newspapers under the sheeting or a sheet of polythene. Shake up the fabric paint bottles. Paint in the colours, working directly from the bottle. Mix colours with white to get pastel shades. You can paint colours over each other and near to each other without them bleeding but you must wash the brush in clean cold water between each colour.

Leave the painted fabric to dry, hanging it up if possible.

Fixing the colour Set the iron to hot. Spread the painted fabric and lay a clean cotton cloth on top. Iron over the painting for at least 2 minutes. This will set the colour into the fabric. Rinse the fabric in cold water, then wash in hot, soapy suds. Rinse carefully and hang the fabric to dry. Iron it smooth. You can now start to make the owl.

Making up the owl Cut out the four ears and the four feet, leaving a seam allowance of 12mm (½in) all round. Stitch them together in pairs from the wrong side. Turn to the right side. Stuff the feet and oversew the ends. Make a small pleat in each ear and baste the pleat. Cut out the two body pieces with the same seam allowance all round. Baste the ears to one body piece, matching raw edges. Lay the second body piece

Fabric painting

Materials required

Sheeting and some kind of filling
Dylon fabric paints
Sewing threads

Tools you will need

Scissors
Ruler, chalk
Soft brush
Needles, pins
Sewing machine
Pattern paper and pencil

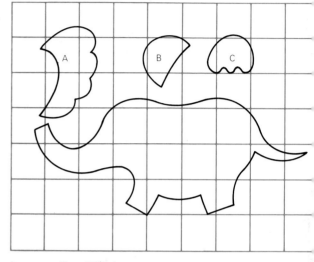

1 square = 40mm (1½in).
A: *elephant ear* B: *owl ear* C: *owl foot*

on top, right side down. Machine stitch, leaving an opening in the under-body seam for filling.

Turn the body to the right side and fill, stuffing rather loosely. Pin the feet into the underbody seam and oversew the seam to close it.

Elephant cushion

Making an elephant Draw up the elephant body shape and the ear shape. Cut out the paper shapes and lay them on sheeting. (One of the elephants illustrated is made from white sheeting, the other was made from a piece of pink sheeting.)

Draw round the shapes, twice for the elephant body, four times for the ears. Paint the design on the sheeting in the same way as for the owl. Dry, and set the colour painting, then rinse, wash and dry the fabric, iron it smooth. Make up a pair of ears, turn to the right side and oversew the seams. Stitch two body pieces together, leaving the under-body open for filling. Turn to the right side and fill.

Close the seam. Stitch on the ears with small slip stitches.

Other ways with ears and feet The ears and feet need not be drawn out and painted on sheeting. Use plain coloured fabric, and use the drawn up pattern to cut out the shapes, remembering to add 12mm (½in) seam allowance all round. White sheeting can of course be dyed with cold water or hot water dyes to produce plain coloured fabrics.

47

Wood crafts

Wood craft, once the accepted hobby for men only, is becoming popular with more and more women. Having got over their fears of hammers, saws and chisels women find that they can saw and shape, glue and pin as comfortably as they cut fabric and sew pieces together.

The tools you will need

Once you get into wood craft, you will add to your collection of tools. To start, you need only a few basic tools. The following are what you need to make the three projects in this chapter, the wall measure, the spice rack and the rocker cradle.

Saws There are three basic types of saw, big handsaws for cutting up lengths of timber, saws for cutting joints and for finer work, and saws for cutting curves and shapes.

The first type includes cross-cut saws, rip saws and panel saws. The second type are the tenon saws and dovetail saws. The third type includes coping saws, bow saws, padsaws and fretsaws.

For the three projects, you need a tenon saw. (A coping saw would also be useful but you can do without it if you want to keep your initial outlay of money to the minimum.)

Surforms Surforms are lightweight, easy-to-handle tools with rasping teeth and they are used for shaping the surface of wood. The finish is a bit rough and has to be smoothed afterwards with sandpaper. Practise using a surform tool on scrap pieces of wood until you get used to the action and can get the effect you want quickly and smoothly.

Drilling holes and punching A wheelbrace is a kind of hand drill. It is slower than an electric drill but easier to use and you will have more control over it. Chucks fitted to wheelbraces have three self-centering jaws to take drill bits or countersinks (for countersunk screws).

Nail punch Nail punches, or pin punches, as they are sometimes called, are used for driving headless nails or panel pins below the surface of the wood. You fill the hole with wood filler and when it is painted over, the fixing is almost invisible.

Screwdriver When you are screwing in a screw, you must always use a screwdriver whose tip exactly fits the slot in the screwhead. Too wide a tip will damage the wood as you screw in and too narrow will spoil the screw slot. For making the spice rack where No. 6 25mm (1in) screws are used, you will need a screwdriver with a tip 5mm (¼in) across. Choose the cabinet or London pattern screwdrivers.

Hammer There are different types of hammers for different jobs. For hammering in panel pins, a pin hammer is sufficient. If you are going to do more woodwork, you might as well have a slightly heavier hammer and choose a cross-pein type which will be used for both pins and tacks.

How-tall-am-I measure

The measure is designed to be hung on the wall so that all the children in the family can stand against it and see who is growing fastest. Make marker arrows from plastic seed markers, cut to a point. Attach a small 'sticky fixer', which is sticky on both sides to the back of the arrow. Make one for each child in the family. The child's name can be written on the arrow with a chinagraph pencil and then attached to the measure.

To start the measure Cut the back batten to 112cm (3ft 8in). Mark rounded corners on the top end, using a large coin. Cut off the corners as closely as possible using the tenon saw. Round off the corners with the surform tool. Finally, glasspaper all edges on the batten to make them smooth. Use the hand drill to make a hole for the nail to support the measure 25mm (1in) from the top end.

Making the measuring boards Cut ten boards, each 180mm (7in) long. Mark rounded corners using a coin. Cut round the corners, as closely as possible, with the tenon saw. Use the surform tool to round off and then finish all edges with glasspaper.

Fixing the measuring boards The first board goes onto the batten at the bottom end, 43mm (1¾in) from the end. Spread adhesive on the batten and immediately position the board. Pin

Measure

Materials required

Softwood (pine) back batten;
   115cm × 50mm × 12mm (3ft 9in
   × 2in × ½in)
For measure boards, piece 180cm
   × 100mm × 12mm (6ft × 4in ×
   ½in)
Woodworking adhesive
Glasspaper No. 1 grade
Panel pins 19mm (¾in)
Plastic wood
Red enamel paint (optional)
Clear polyurethane varnish
Rub-on numbers, transfers

Tools you will need

Tenon saw
Surform tool
Hand drill, 4mm twist drill
Hammer
Nail punch
Try square, ruler, pencil
Varnishing brush

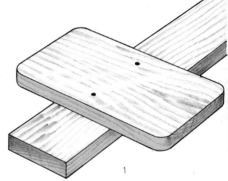

1

the board to the batten (*diagram 1*). Use the nail punch to sink the pin heads about 2mm below the surface of the wood. Fill the hole with plastic wood, smooth off. Position the next board, butting right up against the first. Position all ten boards in the same way.

Decorating the measure You can either paint the batten red or leave it plain varnished.

Rub down numbers have been used on the board illustrated. They are approximately 25mm (1in) deep and on the paper backing sheet will be identified as 72pt. You will need numbers 2 to 9, six 1's and eleven 0's.

Measure and mark a line on each board so that the lines on the ten boards are exactly 100mm (4in) apart. The lines can then be painted in black or marked in black ink. Alternatively, you can use rub-down colour which is sold in sheets in art shops. You simply cut a strip from the sheet to the measurements of the line and then rub it down onto the wood, lifting off the paper backing afterwards.

Finishing the measure Give the measure two or three coats of varnish, letting each coat dry before applying the next. Apply decal transfers if you like. Alternatively, you may prefer to cut pictures or decorations from children's books. Glue these to the measure and varnish when the glue has completely dried.

The measure should be fixed to the wall with a nail through the hole at the top. The nail should be 150cm (4ft 11in) from the ground.

49

Spice rack

Spice rack

Materials required

Softwood (pine)
Piece 600mm × 65mm × 12mm (2ft × 2½in × ½in) for the sides and base
Piece 380mm × 150mm × 12mm (15in × 6in × ½in) for the back
Dowelling 800mm × 12mm (2ft 8in × ½in)
Glasspaper No. 1 grade
Panel pins: 1 packet 35mm (1⅜in), 1 packet 25mm (1in)
2 mirror plates with screws
3 countersunk screws, No. 6 25mm (1in)

Plastic wood or wood filler
Woodworking adhesive
Polyurethane varnish

Tools you will need

Tenon saw
Surform tool
Hammer
Nail punch
Wheelbrace and 3mm (⅛in) bit
Screwdriver
Ruler, pencil
Varnishing brush

This neat-looking kitchen rack would make a splendid gift for a girl or boy just starting up their first bedsitter home — or an inexpensive wedding present. The overall length is 350mm (14in) by 65mm (2½in) wide.

To start the rack Study *diagram 1* first so that you can see exactly how to put the various pieces together. Cut the base first. Mark the middle of the longer piece of wood and then measure out the base of the rack — 300mm long (12in). From this measure the two side pieces, 80mm (3⅛in) long as in *diagram 2*. Cut on the pencilled lines. Smooth the three pieces with glasspaper.

Cut the dowel rod into two pieces, exactly the length of the base piece 300mm (12in) long.

Mark the position of the top dowel on the side pieces, 10mm (⁷/₁₆in) from the top edge and the second rod, 10mm (⁷/₁₆in) below this.

Mark also the position of the base 10mm (⁷/₁₆in) from the bottom edge (*diagram 3*).

Assemble this unit. Make holes for the 35mm (1⅜in) panel pins in the side pieces as shown in *diagram 1*. Spread glue on the surfaces to be joined and place them together immediately. Fix in place with panel pins. Wipe away any glue which has seeped out.

Leave to dry.

Back board The wood for the back board should now be cut to a length of 350mm (14in). Draw curves on the corners using a jar top. Saw off the excess wood and shape with the surform tool. Smooth off with glasspaper. Place the front unit on the back board and pencil in its position as shown in *diagram 4*. Drill 3 screwholes into the back board from the back. Spread glue on the front unit and apply to the back board. Screw the rack together. Fill the screw indentations with wood filler.

Attach the two mirror plates. Give the whole unit three coats of polyurethane varnish for a durable finish.

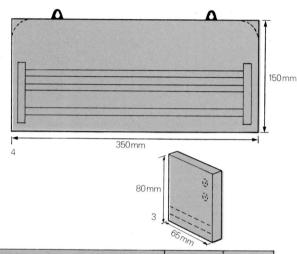

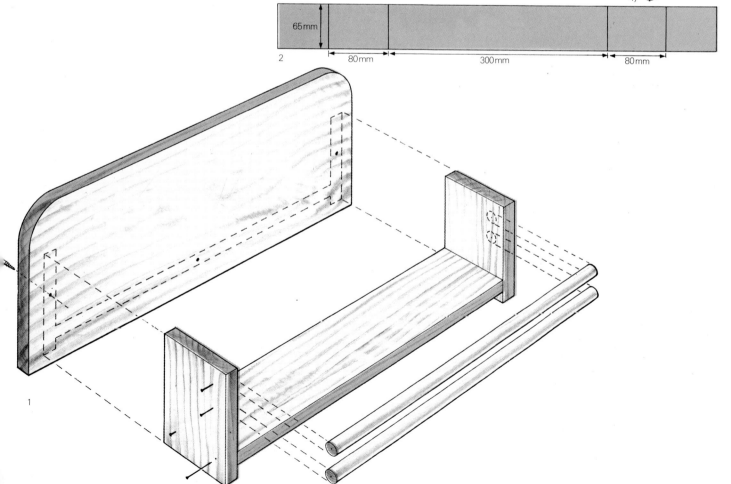

Doll's cradle

This charming little rocking cradle would make a wonderful gift for a little girl, complete with its own lace-trimmed coverlet and pillow. The overall length of the cradle is approximately 355mm (14in).

To start the cradle From *diagram 1*, draw up a pattern for the headboard and footboard. The scale of the diagram is 1 square to 50mm (2in). If you cannot obtain squared paper, draw an area 250mm × 200mm (10in × 8in) and divide it into 50mm (2in) squares. Copy the outline on your squared area. Trace off the two pattern shapes. Cut the paper patterns out. Take the piece of wood measuring 600mm × 180mm (2ft × 7in) and, marking the middle with a pencil line, cut it into two pieces.

Using a piece of carbon paper, draw the cradle ends onto the two pieces. Saw off the waste wood round the shapes and then finish the shaping with the surform tool. (If you have access to a wood vice, you will find surform shaping far easier to do.)

If you have a coping saw, use this for shaping the cradle ends instead of the surform tool. Finish the wood off smoothly with glasspaper.

Sides and bearers Study *diagram 2* at this point so that you can see what you are putting together next. Cut the second piece of wood to make two pieces 330mm × 80mm (13in × 3⅛in). Cut the moulding to make two bearers of exactly the same length.

Spread glue along one side of a bearer and place immediately in position on the cradle side as in *diagram 2*. Immediately make three holes for the 15mm (⅝in) panel pins using the hammer and nail punch.

Hammer in the panel pins, sinking them

Doll's cradle

Materials required

Softwood (pine)
Piece 600mm × 180mm × 12mm (2ft × 7in × ½in)
Piece 700mm × 80mm × 12mm (2ft 4in × 3⅛in × ½in)
Moulding, 700mm (2ft 4in) of 1cm × 1cm (standard size)
Hardboard for base, 180mm × 330mm (7¼in × 13in)
Panel pins: packet 15mm (⅝in), packet 35mm (1⅜in) sizes
Woodworking adhesive
Plastic wood or wood filler
Polyurethane varnish
Glasspaper No. 1 grade

Tools you will need

Tenon saw
Surform tool (or coping saw)
Hammer
Nail punch
Ruler, pencil, squared paper or tracing paper, carbon paper
Varnishing brush

1 square = 50 mm (2 in)

slightly below the surface of the wood. Wipe away any glue which has seeped out now. Glue and pin the other cradle side in the same way. Fill the holes of the panel pins with wood filler. Sand to finish when dry.

Putting on the cradle ends Lay the headboard on the work surface and stand the sides on it. Mark the position they will be in with a pencil. Do the same on the footboard. Make holes for the panel pins.

Spread glue on the cradle sides ends and press to the cradle headboard. Hammer in 35mm (1⅜in) panel pins to join footboard and sides. Do the same to join the footboard as shown in *diagram 2*. Fill the pin holes and sandpaper smooth.

Leave to dry. Brush away all dust and give the cradle 3 coats of clear varnish. Decorate the

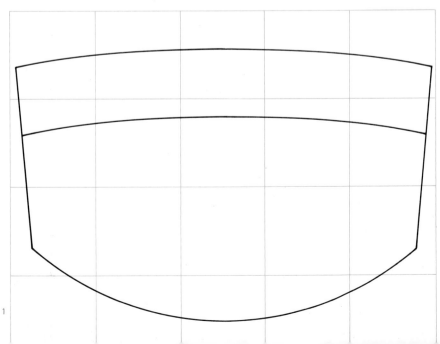

1

headboard and footboard with decal transfers if you like.

Cut the hardboard (mattress support) to fit on the bearers.

Bedcover and pillow The bedcover and pillow are both made in the same way. For each one cut two pieces of cotton fabric the same size and just large enough to fit the cradle. Cut a length of lace edging long enough to go round all four sides. Join the ends of the lace. Pin round one piece of fabric, on the right side, matching the edges. Pin and then baste the second piece on top, right side down. Stitch on three sides and part of the fourth, leaving just enough of the seam open to turn to the right side.

Turn right side out, stuff with cotton wool or kapok and finish off the open seam with oversewing or slip stitches.

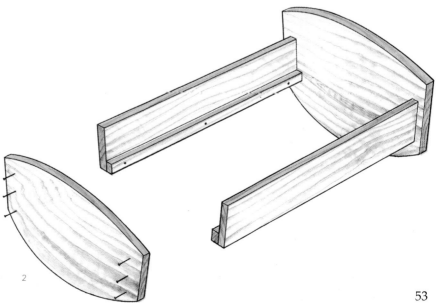

2

Felt and fabric

Felt is a lovely material to make things with. It cuts easily and cleanly and only the simplest sewing is needed to join felt pieces together. The colours of felts are fantastic — they will inspire you to try all kinds of colour effects!

Felt can be used for collage pictures, for appliqué, for patchwork: it can be embroidered, painted on and beaded. It makes bright, colourful clothes, bags, jewellery, slippers, hats, belts, toys of every kind — as well as hundreds of pretty and useful home accessories. The only thing you cannot do with felt is wash it — but it drycleans perfectly well.

Fabrics, woven or knitted, need more sewing techniques to put pieces together. When you are choosing fabrics to make gifts, consider the home that the item is going into and, if you can, select something that is going to suit the furnishing style and the general colour scheme. Flower prints and plain fabrics will match most traditional furnishing schemes. Modern schemes will always accept accessories in plain colour textured fabrics.

A swing needle sewing machine will make fabric crafts much easier and pleasanter but if you want to sew by hand, most of the gifts in this chapter could be made in that way. When you are sewing heavy fabrics, you will need heavy duty needles and threads.

Bags of money!

These little money bags are the easiest of things to make. They are simply two shaped pieces of felt stitched together with running stitches with a hole in the top so that a coin can be put inside. **To make the bags** Trace the bell shape in *diagram 1*. Cut out the shape and use it for a paper pattern. Pin it to a single piece of felt and cut out. Re-pin to a second piece and cut out.

Join the two pieces together with tiny running stitches using a closely matching thread. Leave the top open for the coin as shown in *diagram 1*. Thread a needle with a piece of gold gift cord. Make a loop through the back of the bag near the top edge. Knot the ends. Cut out motifs etc., and glue them to the front of the bag.

To make the ball, draw a circle 50mm (2in) in diameter. Copy the top of the ball from the photograph and use this shape as a pattern.

To make the tree, draw an equilateral triangle, each side measuring 62mm (2½in). Copy the photograph to make the trunk and cut one trunk and two tree shapes in different coloured felts. Sew the trunk in position between the two tree shapes.

Money bags

Materials required

Felt squares, felt scraps
Matching sewing threads
Gift pack cords
Clear all-purpose adhesive

Tools you will need

Tracing paper, pencil
Scissors, needles

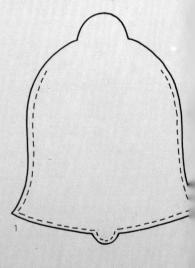

1

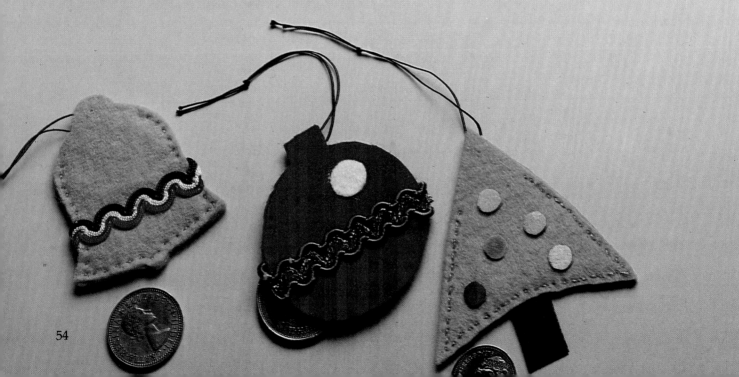

Thimble pips

These pretty little pip-shaped containers are for keeping thimbles in. Perhaps they are not very practical but they do make a charming accessory for a sewing basket and friends who like to sew will love having a thimble pip. The pip opens by squeezing the ends together and the basic shape can be made to look like different kinds of animals and birds by adding ears and tails. The yellow pip is made of felt and decorated with flowers. The blue pip is made of a silky fabric and is decorated with a silver button and beads. Thimble pips make very good bazaar items and are an opportunity for you to use your imagination and colour sense.

The basic technique Trace off the shape from *diagram 2*. Rub a soft pencil over the wrong side of the tracing and draw the pips shape down onto the thin card. For one pip you will need six card shapes. Cut them out. Before cutting the fabric out, you must decide how you are going to decorate the pip (see *Decorating thimble pips*). When you have done this, hold a card pip on the fabric and cut out 6mm (¼in) away from the card. Cut three in the cover fabric and three in a different colour fabric for a lining.

The next stage involves mounting the fabric on the card. Smear a very little adhesive on the extreme edges of the fabric shape on the wrong side. Lay the card shape on the fabric and turn the edges on to the card. You may have to snip into the edges of the fabric to make it turn neatly. From the right side, the edges must be absolutely smooth. Prepare all six pip shapes and leave to dry under a sheet of white paper with a weight on top — a heavy book will do. Leave them to dry for a while.

Glueing shapes together Glue one lining pip to a cover pip shape and leave the three pip shapes to dry under a weight.

When they are quite dry, they are ready to sew together.

Sewing the pips Thread a needle with 2 strands of embroidery thread. Hold two pip shapes together, lining sides together and work Cretan stitch, shown in *diagram 3*, to join them. Join the third shape in the same way, leaving the top of the pip open.

☐ HOW TO WORK CRETAN STITCH Bring the needle through at A and, with the thread above the needle, insert the needle at B and bring it out at the edge on C.

With the thread below the needle, insert the needle at D and bring it through at E. Continue as from point A.

Decorating thimble pips If you are going to embroider pips, work the embroidery on the cover fabric before cutting it out. Appliqué motifs, such as flowers or beads, can be glued on after the pip is finished.

Making the thimble pips illustrated

Mouse pip The mouse is made of a pink, silky fabric and the ears and tail are cut from scraps of black suede. The nose is embroidered and the eyes are black beads stitched to the pip.

White rabbit The body is covered in a white, twilled fabric and the nose is embroidered. Red beads make the eyes and the ears are cut from pink and white felt and glued, then stitched to the pip. The tail is a pompon of pink wool yarn. To make a pompon, cut a circle of card 25mm (1in) in diameter and snip a hole in the centre. Thread a needle with yarn and bind the yarn over and over the card ring until the hole is filled. Snip into the yarn on the edge of the ring. Before tearing the card ring away from the wool, tie a piece of thread round the middle of the ball very tightly. Roll the ball in your hands to make it round and then trim it all over with scissors to make a small, tight pompon. Stitch to the pip.

Yellow felt pip The yellow pip was put together with three strands of embroidery thread so that the Cretan stitch embroidery becomes a design feature. Cut out felt shapes and stick on.

Blue, beaded pip The leaf embroidery was worked in stem stitch before the fabric was cut out. The silvery flower is a button with tiny beads stitched into the petals. The bead button was sewn to the pip shape when the fabric had been mounted on the card but before the outer shape was glued to the liner shape. Green embroidery thread has been used for the joining stitches.

Thimble pips

Materials required

Thin flexible card
Clear, all-purpose adhesive
Fabric scraps: choose thin, firm fabrics or felt
Trimmings: felt scraps, beads, buttons, knitting wool, embroidery threads, sequins etc.
Matching sewing threads

Tools you will need

Tracing paper, pencil
Paper scissors, fabric scissors
Sewing needle, embroidery needle

Pencil holders

Pencil holders, made of felt, make very good gifts for children of all ages. The green folder is for an older child; the folder will hold six pens or pencils, erasers, ruler etc., and also has places for geometry equipment.

The pencil-shaped case is very individual and will hold a lot of pens and pencils. It can be closed with either a zipper or press studs, as you like. The tiny butterfly-trimmed case is for holding coloured crayons and would make a good take-to-the-party gift.

Crayon case

To make it Cut two squares of felt, 112mm × 112mm (4½in × 4½in). Turn a 12mm (½in) hem on the top edge of both. Machine stitch. Place the two pieces together, stitched hems to the outside and stitch on three sides to make the case. Trim the seam allowance to half. Stitch two press studs to close the case. Cut out a butterfly motif (*diagram 1*) in a contrasting felt and glue to the case. Stitch beads or sequins on the wings if desired.

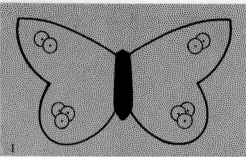

Pencil case

To make it Cut the large square into two pieces. To cut the pencil point, measure up from the bottom 15cm (6in) on both long sides. Measure and mark the middle of the top edge. Chalk a line from the sides to the middle point. Cut off the triangles (*diagram 2*). Copy the shapes in *diagram 3* for the wood part and the point of the pencil, enlarge these shapes to fit the pointed end of the pencil case and make paper patterns for both shapes. Using the patterns, cut both shapes from felt, twice.

If you are using a zipper fastening, stitch the zipper in now, between the two main pencil pieces. (Press fasteners can be stitched on later.) Pin and baste the wood shapes to both pencil shapes and then baste the point shape to both. Cut and baste a length of tape to the insides of the pencil case opening. This is where the snap fasteners will go. Machine stitch the tape.

Baste the two pencil shapes together, right sides out. Machine stitch all round the point, down the long side and across the bottom. Sew on snap fasteners to close.

Decorating the case You can leave the pencil case just as it is or cut out felt letters to make the owner's name. Glue the letters to the case. To make the pencil look more realistic, work stem stitch along the length of the case, from the points of the wood part.

Crayon case

Materials required

Felt 224mm × 112mm (9in × 4½in)
Small piece felt in contrasting colour
2 press studs
Clear all-purpose adhesive
Trimmings: beads, sequins etc.
Sewing thread

Tools you will need

Scissors
Needles
Sewing machine
Tape measure

From the left: Pencil case, Pencil folder, Crayon case

Pencil case

Materials required

Felt in main colour 250mm (10in) square
Felt in second colour for wood part 100mm (4in) square
Scrap for the lead part of the pencil
Stranded embroidery thread
Snap fasteners or zipper
Length of tape (if using snap fasteners)

Tools you will need

Scissors
Tape measure
Chalk
Tracing paper, pencil
Pins, needles
Sewing machine

Pencil folder

To make it Cut a piece of felt 33cm deep by 84cm (13in × 33in). Fold it across the middle and machine stitch on all four sides. The piece now measures 33cm × 42cm (13in × 16½in).

Cut three strips of felt 15mm (⅝in) wide and 44.5cm (17½in) long. Cut one end into a point on each strip. Pin and then baste the three strips across the middle of the folder so that pencils, rulers, etc., can be slipped under the strips.

When you have planned and basted the strips into position, mark the stitching lines with basting threads. Machine stitch across the three strips to secure them. Remove the basting. At the right hand side of the case, cut two narrow strips of felt for button loops. Pin them under the ends of the two outer strips.

Trim off any excess felt and then machine stitch across the ends of the three strips, machining over the previous stitching line.

On the outside of the case, sew on the buttons, 17cm (6¾in) from the edge and in line with the loops, so that when the pencil folder is folded from the left hand end, the buttons meet the loops.

Decorate the outside of the folder with felt flower shapes or with initials. Cut a strip of felt with pinking shears and glue to the botton loop edge to hide the machine stitching.

Pencil folder

Materials required

Green felt 45cm × 90cm (18in × 36in)
Scraps for decoration
2 buttons, sewing thread
Fabric adhesive

Tools you will need

Scissors, tape measure
Pins, needles
Sewing machine
Pinking shears

Ribbon cushions

Here are two unusual cushions to make with ribbons. The striped cushion is a variation of appliqué. The other is an example of an old needlecraft, ribbon weaving.

Appliqué cushion

To make the appliqué Plan the arrangement of ribbons first. Pin strips diagonally across one square of the fabric. Cut the ends of the ribbons to align with the fabric square sides.

When you are pleased with the arrangement, remove the ribbons, keeping them in the same order of arrangement, and lay them on a table, so that you can pick up each one as you need it.

The ribbons can be stitched down either with a straight stitch or with a zigzag stitch, as you prefer.

Baste down the two ribbons which lie across the middle. Machine stitch them to the background. Apply the ribbons to each side of the centre, working towards the corners, until the whole square is covered. Dry-press carefully on the wrong side, noting the fibre content of the ribbons. (Ribbons made of some synthetic fibres can melt if the iron is too hot.)

Making up the cushion Trim the ribbon ends if needed. Put the zipper in now, if you are using one. (It is easier to insert a zipper between two flat pieces of fabric!)

Centre the zipper on one side of the cushion. Stitch the cushion together from the wrong side. Press the seams flat, then open. Trim the seam allowance, cut off the corners diagonally. Catch down the zipper tape to the seam allowance.

Piping If you prefer to pipe the cushion edges, baste the piping to the right side of the bottom square, before putting in the zipper. Stitch through all thicknesses of fabric.

Hand appliqué The ribbon strips can be hand sewn if you prefer. Baste strips together and then oversew the edges or work tiny running stitches 3mm (1/8in) from the edge.

Woven cushion

Ribbon weaving was a Victorian needlecraft and it was used to make all kinds of decorative accessories and furnishings from beautiful bedcovers to book covers. The cushion illustrated demonstrates the easiest method, a simple basket weave, but a variety of effects can be achieved by various weaves. If you would like to experiment with this technique, cut strips of coloured paper and see what interesting patterns can be built up. Ribbon, which used to be fairly inexpensive, is now almost a luxury material so this is not a way of making a cheap gift. However, there is no reason why strips of dressmaking fabric, left over from a dressmaking session, should not be used. Cut the strips on the true bias (on the cross) and pull them slightly as you work so that the raw edges are pulled to the underside of the work. Fabrics which ravel easily might have to be finished with zigzag stitching on the cut edges.

Note: Although ribbons are sold to certain

Appliqué cushion

Materials required

Square cushion pad
Fabric for cushion: 2 squares 25mm (1in) larger than pad
Assorted ribbons and braids 7m (7yd) approximately
Zipper 75mm (3in) shorter than side of cushion pad or press fasteners on tape
Matching sewing threads
Basting thread

Tools you will need

Sewing machine
Sewing needles
Pins
Scissors

Woven cushion

Materials required

Cushion pad
Backing fabric
Calico
Card
Strong thread, sewing thread
Ribbons, 25mm (1in) wide, in 2 contrasting colours

Tools you will need

Needles, pins
Pencil
Scissors
Sewing machine

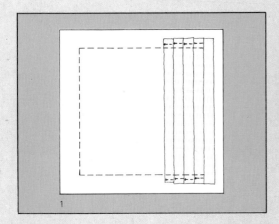

1

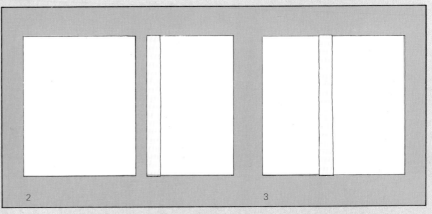

2   3

widths, different types of ribbon may vary although they are sold as being of the same width. This discrepancy can make a difference to the number of strips needed to make up a cushion, so be sure that you allow sufficient. Wider ribbons would of course take up less yardage.

The technique The cushion must have an extra 25mm (1in) all round for seams. To achieve this, cut the ribbons 50mm (2in) longer than the finished cushion width and depth. You will then also need 1 extra strip of ribbon on each side of the cushion to weave into the ribbon ends on the edges (*diagram 1*).

Cover a piece of card with the calico, lacing the edges at the back with strong thread.

Mark out the area you will be weaving in pencil, allowing 25mm (1in), or one ribbon width, as a seam allowance all round.

Pin the ends of lengths of ribbon of one colour, sides touching on the calico, keeping them as smooth as possible. Cut ribbons in the second colour, weave them in and out, pinning the ends. When all the ribbons are pinned, go over the first lot again, adjusting them and repinning where necessary for a smooth effect. Thread a needle with a matching thread and work small running stitches, sewing the ribbons to the backing. Cut the lacing threads and remove the backing card from the calico. Machine stitch all round the weaving, stitching 3mm (⅛in) from the seam line. Trim the calico so that there is 25mm (1in) seam allowance all round. Make up the cushion in the usual way, inserting piping if you desire. Trim the seam allowance back to 6mm (¼in).

LEFT: *Appliqué cushion*
BELOW: *Woven cushion*

Finishing the cushion This type of cushion cover would be better with an envelope finish instead of the usual zipper or press fastener closure.

To make this, cut the backing fabric to the depth of the cushion plus 25mm (1in) seam allowance by the width plus 150mm (6in). Cut the fabric into two pieces, one 75mm (3in) wider than the other. Turn a narrow hem on one piece. Trim the other with a piece of ribbon (*diagram 2*). Lay the two pieces overlapping so that they match the size of the cushion (*diagram 3*). Baste them together and then make up the cushion in the usual way. When the cushion is finished, the ribbon-trimmed edge is open and the cushion pad is slipped in through the opening.

Ideas for using ribbon weaving

Use sale bargains of short lengths of superb ribbons to make up a small area of weaving. Turn a neat hem to the wrong side and use the weaving as a piece of brilliant appliqué on a velvet cushion cover. Or, weave a square of ribbons including strips of the cushion fabric. Make up a cushion front and back. Cut a hole in the cushion front. Turn a narrow hem. Pin and then machine stitch the weaving behind the 'window'.

Covered matchboxes

Pretty matchboxes

For a quick-to-make and inexpensive gift, mount two, three or four boxes of matches on card covered with fabric. It is simple to do and the finished effect is attractive. Boxes of matches always make acceptable gifts, particularly if you choose a covering fabric to suit the room where the matches will be used. A pretty cotton print would turn the matches into a sitting room accessory, while a plain, dark fabric might be used for a man's desk. Vinyl or a plasticised cotton is easily wiped clean and would be ideal for kitchen matches.

Mounting the matchboxes Group two, three or four boxes on a piece of stiff cardboard (*diagram 1* shows the different positions of the boxes illustrated). When a pleasing arrangement has been achieved, draw round the outline of the grouped boxes making sure that they do not move. Cut out the shape with a sharp knife or scissors. Place the shape on another piece of cardboard, draw round it and cut out a second piece.

Using just a smear of adhesive, stick each piece of cardboard to the wrong side of the fabric and then cut out, leaving 12mm (½in) surplus fabric all round. Mitre the corners and clip into the angles (*diagram 2*). Fold the excess fabric over and glue it down to the cardboard.

Glue the matchboxes into position on the wrong side of one piece of covered cardboard. Glue the second piece of covered cardboard on top and press down firmly. Leave the boxes under a weight until quite dry.

Finishing the matchboxes Cut a 62mm (2½in) length of ribbon for each drawer. Remove the matches from the boxes. Fold the ribbon in half lengthways and glue cut ends inside the boxes so that a looped end protrudes as illustrated. Replace the matches in the boxes.

Matchbox bureau

Six large-size matchboxes will make a very useful miniature bureau. On a dressing table, the drawers can be used for small pieces of jewellery, hairgrips, tweezers, nailscissors, safety pins and, perhaps, lengths of ribbon.

A dressmaker would probably use the drawers for all kinds of sewing odds and ends — tape measure, pins, needles, buttons, snap fasteners and so on.

Cover the bureau with a pretty cotton fabric — for a bedroom it could match the curtains.

How to make it Take the trays out of the boxes and glue the sleeves together. While the glue is drying, paint the insides and outsides of the trays with either emulsion paint or poster colour. Measure the front end of one tray carefully. Iron the cotton fabric onto medium-weight adhesive Vilene. On the wrong side of the mounted fabric, draw out 6 shapes to fit the tray ends. Cut out neatly and glue one to each of the tray ends.

Pierce two holes in the tray ends, about 3mm (⅛in) apart. Thread a small button or bead on button thread and pass both ends of the thread through the holes (*diagram 3*). Tie a double knot on the inside of the tray, so that the bead or button is tight against the tray end.

Paint the glued-together outers so that all the wood edges are coloured.

Measure the outer, first the depth from front to back and then all round it. Add 25mm (1in) for overlap.

Draw the area of the bureau cover on the wrong side of the mounted fabric, adding 6mm (¼in) all round. Cut out. Turn the edges to the wrong side and glue down.

Spread fabric glue on the bureau outer right to the edges. Put the fabric on, smoothing it with your fingers and overlap the join underneath. If you want to put little feet under the bureau, glue wooden beads to the underside.

Pretty matchboxes

Materials required

Boxes of matches
Fabric or self-adhesive vinyl to cover
Narrow ribbon
Stiff cardboard
Fabric adhesive

Tools required

Scissors or sharp knife
Card strip for spreading glue

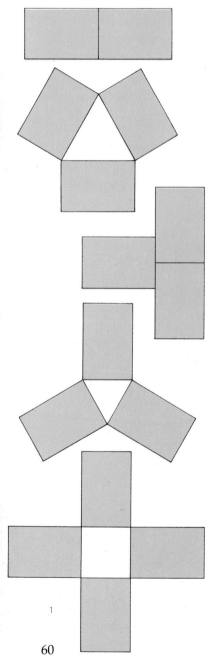

1

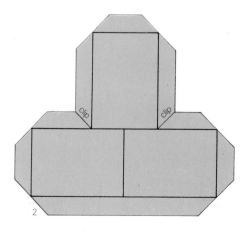

2

Matchbox bureau

Materials required

6 large matchboxes
Emulsion or poster paint
Medium-weight iron-on Vilene
 45cm (½yd)
Cotton fabric, 45cm (½yd) 90cm
 (36in) wide
Clear, all-purpose adhesive
Latex-based fabric glue
6 small buttons or beads
4 large wooden beads (optional)
Button thread

Tools you will need

Scissors
Pencil, ruler
Paint brush

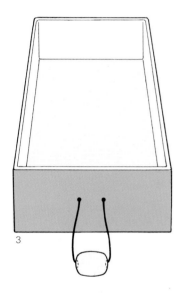

3

Above left: Matchbox bureau
Right: Pretty matchboxes in different arrangements

Doorstep cat

If you have any doubts at all about giving a doorstep cat as a gift, make one for yourself. Everyone who comes to your house will demand one! Children visitors will want to use it for a stool to sit on — and it does the cat no harm at all. Fur fabric makes a real-looking cat but the pattern looks just as effective in a patterned furnishing fabric or a textured fabric such as tweed or corduroy.

Preparing the pattern The pattern (*diagram 1*) is for the cat's body and his ears. Draw a rectangle 25cm (10in) deep × 30cm (12in) wide. Mark and divide it into 5 50mm (2in) squares down and 6 50cm (2in) squares across. Copy the cat's body onto your pattern.

Draw in the ear shape and trace it to make a separate paper pattern.

Cutting the fabric Pin the cat's body pattern to the wrong side of doubled fabric. Chalk round the pattern. Cut out 12mm (½in) away from the chalked line.

Cut a piece of fabric 15cm (6in) wide and 30cm (12in) long. Round off the corners. This is for the cat's base.

Cut out two ears in felt. Cut a strip 23cm × 10cm (9in × 4in) for the cat's tail.

Cut out a cardboard base to the same size and shape as the fabric base.

Making up the cat Cut the strip for the tail in two lengthwise (*diagram 2*). Pin the pieces right sides together. Taper one end of both pieces for about 10cm (4in). Start stitching in the middle of a long side. Stitch round the tip, up the other long side, across the end and down the long side but stop 50mm (2in) from the start.

Trim the seams, turn right side out and stuff the tail, not too tightly. Oversew the seam to close. Pin and then baste the tail to the right side of one cat body. Fold the sides of the ears in and stitch the edges to hold the fold. Pin and then baste the ears to the same body piece (*diagram 3*). Lay the other body piece on top, right side down, and stitch round the body but leaving the base open and a gap in the middle of the back, about 125mm (5in) wide.

Stitch the base to the body. You will have to pleat the body edge a little to make the edges fit.

Bend the cardboard and push it into the base. Put the brick in on top of the cardboard. Start filling, pushing the filling all round the brick and rounding off the cat's body. Fill the head with cotton wool. Close off the open seam with neat slip stitches, turning in the raw edges.

Catch the tail tip to the body, curving it naturally. If you are making a collar, cut a strip of felt to fit the cat's neck about 25mm (1in) wide. Sew the bell to it. Sew the collar round the neck. Sew on the eyes.

Cat cushion

Using the same body pattern, enlarged to 1 square to 75mm (3in), you can make a cushion.

Cut four ear shapes in the same fabric, adding 12mm (½in) seam allowance and make them up in pairs. Make the tail as for the doorstep cat but do not make a base. Embroider eyes and stuff the cushion with Kapok.

Doorstep cat

Materials required

Fabric 45cm (½yd)
Felt for ears
Cotton wool filling for tail and head
Collar or felt for making collar
Small bell
2 pearl buttons for eyes or toy eyes
Cardboard for base
Foam chip filling (or Kapok)
1 house brick

Tools you will need

Paper, pencil
Ruler, scissors

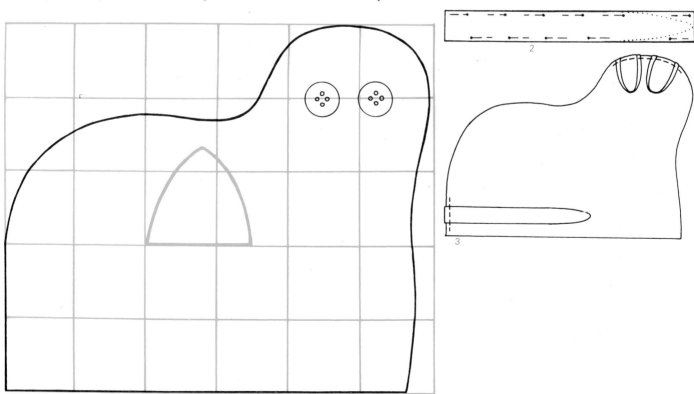

Leather gifts

Leather is a material which appeals to men. It looks good, it has a pleasant feel and wears reasonably well. Leathercraft has a great many applications and techniques which have to be learned but it is a worthwhile and profitable craft because, apart from the basic materials, few essential tools are required and you can do leatherwork at home.

The two items illustrated, a woven belt and a card case, use only the simplest techniques and tools.

Plaited belt

Making up the belt Some leather needs dampening before working but chrome-tanned sheepskin does not.

Spread adhesive along the strips on the wrong side and fold the sides to the middle. Leave to dry.

Fasten the four strips to a work bench, side by side, anchor them with tacks. Mentally number the strips from the left, 1, 2, 3, 4.

Following *diagram 1*, bring 3 over 2. Bring 1 over 3.

Bring 4 under 2 and over 1. Bring 3 over 4. Bring 2 under 1 and over 3. Bring 4 over 2. Bring 1 under 3 and over 4. Bring 2 over 1. Take 3 under 4 and over 2.

This is the method for 4-strand plaiting. Keep the curves of the plaits smooth and even. Plait to the ends of the strip.

Hold the ends together with the bulldog clip. Go over the belt making sure the plaits are smooth. Lay the belt on the table and cut the turnings off the ends with a sharp crafts' knife so that you are working with single thicknesses. Glue the ends together and hammer them flat.

Trace off the shape in *diagram 2*. Use this pattern to cut the two larger strips for one end of the belt. Glue them, wrong sides together over the end of the belt. Leave to dry under a weight. Glue the square-cornered strip to the buckle end.

Machine stitch round the shaped end of the belt through both thicknesses. Machine stitch round the single thickness of the buckle strip. Put the buckle on and push the prong through the middle of the leather. Fold the leather over and glue down to hold the buckle. Punch a single hole in the middle of the other end of the belt.

Polish the belt with a little wax polish to give it a glossy finish.

Plaited belt

Materials required

4 strips of soft leather (chrome-tanned sheepskin), 25mm (1in) wide, cut to the waist measurement plus 50mm (2in) (if pieces have to be joined to get the length, glue them together).
Two strips of leather 80mm × 37mm (3¼in × 1½in)
One strip of leather 62mm × 37mm (2½in × 1½in)
Buckle with 37mm (1½in) bar
Matching button thread
Contact adhesive

Tools you will need

Sharp scissors
Sewing machine and size 16 needle or special spear-pointed leather needle
Tracing paper for patterns
Bulldog clip, hammer, tacks
Ruler, pencil

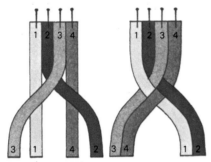

1

2

Card case

Materials required

Soft leather, about 15cm (6 square inches)
Small piece of acetate film
Matching button thread
Contact adhesive

Tools you will need

Sewing machine and size 16 needle or special spear-pointed leather needle
Scissors, blunt darning needle
Ruler and pencil
Tracing paper for pattern

Card case

The card case is for holding a ticket or a pass. The same design could be made as a luggage label holder by adding a thong tie to the open end.

Making up the case Measure the card for which the case is intended. Draw out a rectangle to the size plus 12mm (½in) on the tracing paper. Cut it out. Draw round the outline on the wrong side of the leather. Draw another piece. Draw a window on the second piece to the size of the card. Cut out both pieces of the case.

Using the ruler and blunt darning needle, mark the stitching line 3mm (⅛in) from the edge on both pieces of leather, leaving one short end unmarked. Press down firmly with the needle point to make a crease for the stitches. Cut a piece of acetate to the size of the card plus 3mm (⅛in) all round. Cut out the window in the front piece.

Glue the acetate on the wrong side of the window aperture. Keep the glue carefully to the edges.

Spread glue around the edges to be stitched, on both surfaces of the card case. Press them together to dry. Machine stitch on the creased line on three sides, leaving one short end open.

Map case

Any motorist would appreciate a smart looking map case for the car. You might make a simple key ring tag to match.

To start the map case Cut a piece of vinyl with scissors to 45cm long and 30cm deep (18in × 12in). Lay it, fabric side up, on a flat surface. From the left hand end, mark a line for the flap, 137mm (5½in) from the edge. Mark another line 37mm (1½in) from the edge, inside the flap. Mark and measure a line 25mm (1in) from the top and bottom edges. Mark the tab on the flap 37mm wide by 37mm deep (1½in × 1½in). Round off the corners of the tab and flap, using a large coin as a pattern (*diagram 1*). Cut out the shaded area in the diagram, along the marked lines. On the main body of the map case, mark a line 25mm (1in) from the edge on the top, right hand and bottom edges.

Measure and mark the centre of the top and bottom edge. Cut into the edge up to the line. Make cuts at A and B to remove the corners as shown (*diagram 2*). Using the crafts' knife cut 2 slits for the flap tab on the right hand end of the map case, 75mm (3in) in from the edge, 12mm (½in) apart and 40mm (1⅝in) long. Cut two pieces of acetate film, 250mm deep by 145mm wide (10in × 5¾in).

Making up the case Place the acetate on the fabric side of the map case so that one piece is lined up with the marks A and B and the other with the marked flap line. The pieces of acetate will have a gap between them in the middle of the map case. This is so that the case will fold easily and the maps can be slid in under the film.

The edges of the vinyl are glued down onto the film to hold the pieces in place but this is a job that has to be done slowly and carefully so glue each turning separately and let it dry before going on to the next.

Start with the top edges. Spread glue along the edge of the vinyl (on the fabric surface) and turn it onto the top edge of the acetate film. Press down firmly and leave to dry under a weight — a kitchen weight or a book would be ideal.

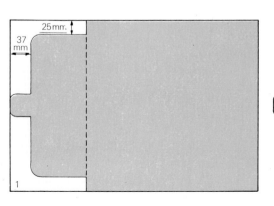

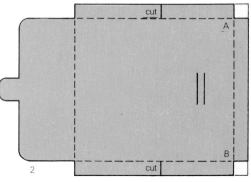

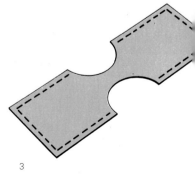

Map case	Car wash mitt	Polishing mitt
Materials required	**Materials required**	**Materials required**
Soft, fabric-backed vinyl, a piece 45cm × 30cm (18in × 12in) Acetate film, 2 pieces 250mm × 145mm (10in × 5¾in) Clear all-purpose adhesive Snap fastener Gold stick-on initials (optional)	Chamois leather 20cm × 20cm (8in × 8in) Foam sheeting 6mm thick, 3 × 20cm squares (¼in thick, 3 × 8in squares) Sewing thread Adhesive tape	Washable fur fabric 2 × 20cm squares (2 × 8in squares) Cotton fabric 2 × 20cm squares (2 × 8in squares) Sewing thread
Tools you will need	**Tools you will need**	
Metal edged ruler Crafts' knife Scissors, tape measure, felt-tipped pen	Tracing paper Pencil Scissors Needle	

Stick down all the edges in turn.

When all the edges are firmly glued, the case is finished. If you prefer a snap fastening rather than a tab, use the hammer-on type and apply the fastener before starting to put in the acetate.

You can personalize the case by attaching stick-on gold initials to the outside of the flap.

Matching key tag

Vinyl can be stitched very easily, using a strong, sharp needle and button thread. Cut a piece of vinyl 120mm × 40mm (4¾ × 1½in). Using a small coin as a guide, cut half-circles out of each side as in *diagram 3*. Fold over a key ring. Stitch on the dotted line, either by sewing machine using a large sized stitch or by hand. Add a gold initial to match the map case.

Car wash mitt

It is not at all easy to find gifts to make for a man. This useful car washing mitt is easy enough for a child to make.

Making the pattern Use a man's glove as a guide for making the pattern. Lay it on paper and draw round the glove, 50mm (2in) away, making the shape longer at the wrist by about 75mm (3in). Refer to the illustration for the general shape. (If you are making the glove for yourself, draw round your hand, 60mm (2½in) away.) Cut out the glove pattern and cut out chamois shape and three foam shapes.

Putting the mitt together Put the chamois piece and one foam piece together. Oversew together along the straight wrist edge. Put the two remaining foam pieces together. Oversew together along the straight wrist edge. Now put the two double-mitt pieces together, chamois side on the inside, facing a foam piece. Oversew all round the curved edge, from one side of the wrist edge to the other. Finish thread securely. Turn the mitt right side out.

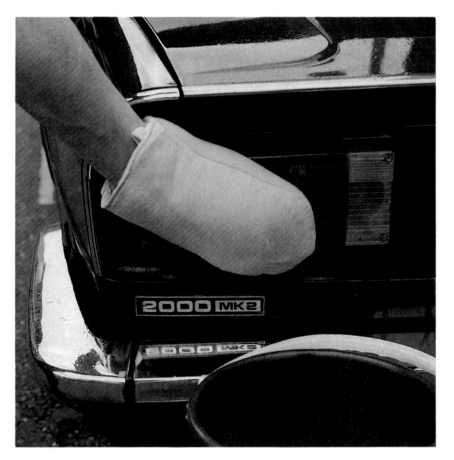

Polishing mitt

You could also make a mitt in fur fabric to polish the car after cleaning.

Make a pattern in the same way as for the Car wash mitt. Cut two shapes from a washable fur fabric and two from cotton fabric, but allow an extra 12mm (½in) all round.

Oversew a fur fabric piece to a cotton piece along the wrist edge. Sew a second pair together. Lay the two mitt pieces together, fur fabric to fur fabric. Work back stitch or machine stitch all round the mitt. Trim the seam allowance to half. Clip into curve so that it turns neatly. Turn the mitt fur side out.

Stitch a small fabric loop to the inside of the wrist.

Sleepy dog toy

Sleepy dog toy

Materials required

Soft fabric, velveteen, needlecord
etc., 1m (1yd)
Scraps of black and bëige felt for
nose and eyes, green felt for a
collar
Kapok filling
Sewing threads

Tools you will need

Paper, pencil, ruler
Scissors, pins, sewing needle
Sewing machine

Most soft toy patterns take time to put together.
This loveable sleepy dog is very easy to make.
The body is an oval and the four floppy legs fit
into the body seam. Sleepy dog sleeps on the
bed all day and makes a cuddly toy at night.

Use a soft fabric such as cotton velveteen or
needlecord for his body and scraps of felt for his
nose and ears. You will also need a lining
material for his ears.

Making the pattern The pattern in *diagram 1* is
to a scale of 1 square to 50mm (2in). Draw a
rectangle 40cm × 75cm (16in × 30in) and mark
and divide it into 50mm (2in) squares.

Copy the pattern pieces onto your squared
paper. Cut out the 6 pattern pieces.

Diagram 2 is a traceoff pattern for the dog's
nose, eyes and eyelashes.

Cutting out Pin the pieces for the leg, ear, head
and body to doubled fabric on the wrong side.
Chalk the outline and cut out, 12mm (½in) away
from the pattern edge. Unpin the leg pattern.
Re-pin to doubled fabric and cut out 2 more legs.
Unpin and re-pin again, until you have eight leg
pieces. Pin the chin pattern to single fabric and
cut out. Cut out 2 black nose pieces and 2
eyelashes in black and 2 eyelids in beige felt.

Re-pin the ear pattern to doubled lining fabric
and cut out, again 12mm (½in) from the pattern
edge.

To make the dog Make up four legs. Stitch two
leg pieces together on the wrong side. Turn,
stuff the paws only and put the four legs aside.

Make up the tail. Stuff a little and put aside.
Stitch two head pieces together. Seam the chin
piece to the head pieces, leaving the neck open.
Make up two ears from one fabric piece and one
lining piece. Turn ears to the right side and press
lightly. Pleat the ends of the ears and baste to
hold the pleat.

Cut a slit in the head on both sides, as marked,
to take the ears. Turn in a narrow hem and hem
the ears into the head.

Pin, and then baste the legs to the right side of
the body piece, folding the legs to the middle of
the body. Baste the tail to the body piece. Lay the
second body piece on top face down. Machine
stitch through all thicknesses leaving the neck
open. (If you find the body difficult to stitch by
machine, stitch by hand using backstitches.)

Turn the body to the right side and stuff
firmly. Sew the head to the body at the neck
using slip stitches.

Sew the nose to the head with small hemming
stitches. Sew the eyelids and eyelashes to each
side of the head.

Make a green felt collar and stitch it around
the dog's neck.

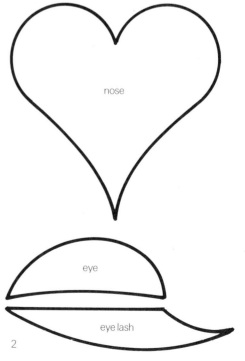

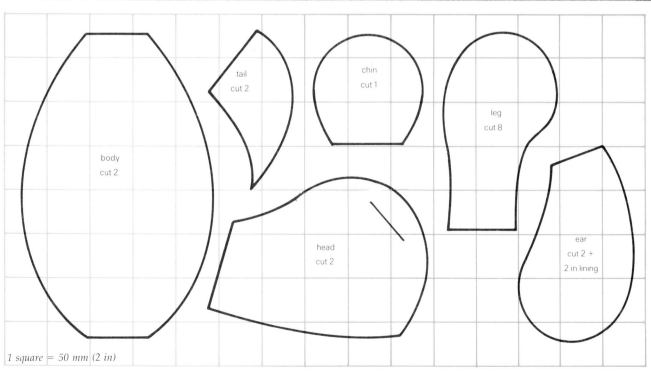

tail
cut 2

chin
cut 1

leg
cut 8

body
cut 2

head
cut 2

ear
cut 2 +
2 in lining

1 square = 50 mm (2 in)

Pyjama case bunny

Make this bunny in a fleecy fabric — such as Courtelle or cotton jersey — so that he is cuddly and soft and will stand up to being a bedtime toy as well as a pyjama case. For a washable bunny, use cotton fabric for the ears lining and the eyes and nose.

Making the pattern *Diagram 1* is the pattern for the bunny's body. The scale is 1 square to 25mm (1in). Draw the pattern on squared paper or mark out an area 450mm square (18in square) and mark it into 25mm (1in) squares. Copy the pattern pieces onto the area. Cut out the pieces, marking in the balance marks and the fold lines. You will probably find it easier if you use a pair of pencil compasses to draw curves. The small * on each pattern piece shows where the point of the compasses should be placed.

Cutting out Pin the body pattern to single fabric and cut out. Fold the fabric and pin out the head, ear, upper foot and sole pieces. Cut out so that there are two of each piece. Pin out the paw piece and cut two and then, re-pin and cut two more so that you have four paw pieces. Pin the ear pattern to doubled pink felt and cut out two ears. Re-pin the ear pattern to the buckram and cut out two buckram ears. Trim the buckram ears 3mm (⅛in) all round.

Making up the body Fold the body piece, fleecy sides together, on the broken line on the pattern. The edges overlap for the centre back opening. Baste the centre back seam. Machine stitch the seam from the point x on the pattern to the bottom edge. All seams are 6mm (¼in). Machine stitch across the bottom edge of the body, working from the wrong side. Work running stitches round the top edge to gather it.

Making up the ears Place a fleece ear piece and a felt ear piece together, right sides facing and stitch together, taking a 6mm (¼in) seam and leaving the bottom edge open. Trim and clip the seam allowance. Turn to the right side. Make up two ears in the same way. Slip the buckram ear pieces inside. Baste across the open end to hold the buckram in position.

Making up the head Lay one head piece, fleecy side up, and position the ears on the head piece, cut edges matching. Pin. Lay the second head piece on top, fleecy side down, and baste through all thicknesses. Machine stitch all round leaving the seam between the notches open. Turn to the right side. Stuff the bunny's head.

Joining head to body Adjust the gathers on the neck edge of the body to fit the neck of the head. Unpick the centre back seam basting and pin the head to the body. Working from the inside of the body, machine stitch. Now hand sew the Velcro

fastening into the back seam. Oversew the neck seam edges to neaten them.

Making up the paws On the upper foot pieces, gather the curved edges. With right sides facing, pin the gathered edges to the curved edge of the sole pieces, adjusting the gathering to fit. Machine stitch, working from the sole side of the foot. Turn inside out and stuff both feet. Turn in a narrow hem on the straight edges and slip stitch. Slip stitch the feet to the body. In the same way, sew two paw pieces together, leaving the straight edge open. Stuff, turn a narrow hem on the edges and then slip stitch together, pulling up the stitches slightly to gather. Slip stitch the paws to the body side seams, 25mm (1in) below the neck seam.

Bunny's features Trace off the life-size eye and nose shapes (*diagram 2*). Cut out the paper patterns and pin to felt. Cut out two black eyes and one pink nose.

Sew the eyes and nose to the bunny's face with hemming stitches.

The woolly hair Cut a piece of cardboard 15cm × 6.25cm (6in × 2½in). Wind the knitting wool round the cardboard about 30 times. Thread a piece of wool on a darning needle and push the needle along one edge of the card, under the

Pyjama case bunny

Materials required

Fleece-surfaced fabric, 23cm (9in)
Pink felt for the ears, 1 30cm (12in) square
Cotton fabric for pants, 13cm × 17cm (5in × 6¾in)
Fancy ribbon for pant's shoulder straps, 45cm (½yd), 12mm (½in) wide
Scraps of felt, pink and black
White double knitting yarn, 3m (3yd)
Buckram stiffening
Filling, Kapok or foam chips
Narrow, round hat elastic, 90cm (1yd)
Squared paper, 25mm (1in) or tracing paper
Velcro fastening, 15cm (6in)
Sewing threads

Tools you will need

Scissors, pencil compasses
Pencil, ruler, tape measure
Darning needle, pins
Large-eyed needle for wool yarn
Sewing machine

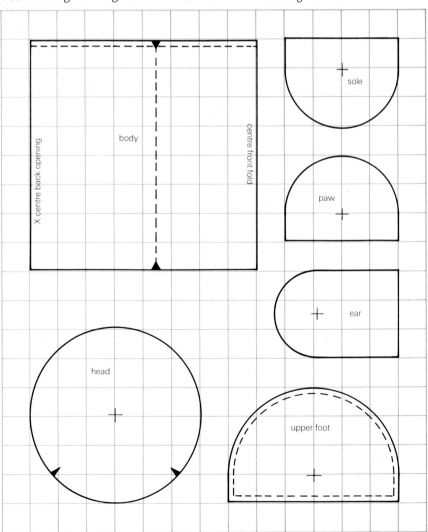

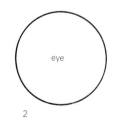

eye

2

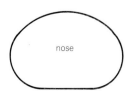

nose

loops of wool, so that you pick up all the loops. Drop the needle off and tie the ends of the wool. Cut another piece of wool and sew the loops of yarn to the bunny's head between the ears.

Dressing the bunny Cut two pieces of cotton 125mm deep × 30cm wide (5in × 12in). Pin them together, right sides facing and machine stitch the short sides taking a 12mm (½in) seam.

Turn a doubled 9mm (⅜in) hem on the top edge and stitch to make a casing for the elastic, leaving a gap in the seam centre back. Measure and mark the middle of the lower edges and stitch together along 25mm (1in) for a trouser gusset, taking an 18mm (¾in) seam. Turn a doubled 9mm (⅜in) hem on each trouser leg and stitch a casing, leaving an opening in the

seam. Run elastic through the waist casing and the leg casings. Fit the trousers on the bunny and knot the elastic ends. Close the casing openings. Cut pieces of ribbon for the shoulder straps and sew to the trousers, back and front. Catch the straps to the bunny's shoulders.

Dressing table set

A co-ordinated dressing table set of tissue box cover, picture frame and waste bin, can be inexpensively made with self-adhesive velour — the quick way to a luxury look. Choose the best braids and trims you can get because it is these touches that make the set look so elegant.

Tissue boxes vary in size so the instructions are given assuming you are taking your own measurements.

To start the box cover Measure the width and length of the tissue box top and add 6mm (¼in) to each measurement.

Measure the long side and a short side and add 6mm (¼in) to each of the measurements. Using these dimensions cut a piece of card for the top of the box, and two pieces for each side.

Take the perforated opening from the top of the box. Lay it on the wrong side of the card top and draw round it. Cut the shape out with the knife. Cut pieces of the velour paper using the card pieces as patterns. Do not cut the hole in the box top in the velour at this stage.

Mount the velour on the card pieces, stripping away the backing from one short end first. Match the corners of the velour to the corners of the card and slowly pull the backing away, smoothing the velour down as you work. Cover the box top in the same way. To cut the hole, use scissors. Cut a hole 12mm (½in) away from the card edges. Snip into the velour all round and then stick the tabs to the wrong side of the card (*diagram 1*).

Putting the box cover together Cut pieces of adhesive tape to the depth of the box. Lay a long side and a short side, side by side wrong sides up and touching, and tape the two pieces together. As you put the tape down, lift one piece of card to form a right angle to the other so that a neat corner join is formed (*diagram 2*). Make up the other two box sides in the same way. Then tape the two pieces together. Tape the box top into position (*diagram 3*).

Edge the box top opening with a narrow trim, glueing it in position.

Cover the seams of the box with braid. Cover the short ends of the box top first and then cut strips of braid long enough to do the corner seams and top in one piece. Slip the cover on to the tissue box. When the tissues are used, the box can be removed from the empty box and used on a new box.

To make the picture frame Set the pencil compasses to 55mm (2¼in) and draw two circles on cardboard with a diameter of 110mm (4½in). Reset the compasses to 30mm (1¼in) and mark a 60mm (2½in) circle in one of the circles. Cut out both circles and then cut out the circular window

in one. You will find it easier to cut out the circles if you use a metal rule and a crafts' knife. Hold the ruler across the circle so that one edge lies on the edge of the circle.

Draw the blade along the edge of the ruler. Move the ruler as shown in *diagram 4a*, and cut again. Work round the circumference of the circle, scoring the edge. If the cardboard is too thick for you to cut right through in one cut, you will find that you can easily complete the cutting out with scissors.

To cut the circular window, draw star lines across the circle and cut along them (*diagram 4b*). Then cut round the edge with blade or scissors.

Cut a circle of the velour paper 115mm (4¾in) in diameter and mount it on the window circle. Cut out the window as you did for the tissue box cover and turn the tabs to the wrong side. Snip into the outer edge and turn to the wrong side. Cover the other circle with velour paper in the same way, snipping into the edge and turning the tabs to the wrong side for a neat finish.

Glue gold braid edging round the outside edge of the frame, on the wrong side, so that the edging shows as illustrated. Cut a circle of acetate film 65mm (2⅝in) across and glue to the wrong side of the window frame. Place the two frame pieces together, right sides out and glue together round the bottom half only, glueing only on the edges. The top half of the frame is open so that a photograph can be slipped between the frame. Glue edging round the window. Make a strut by cutting a strip of card 100mm × 37mm wide (4in × 1½in). Score across one end, 15mm (⅝in) from the end. Cover the strip with velour paper on both sides. Glue firmly to the back of the frame.

To cover the waste bin Measure the circumference of the bin and add 25mm (1in) to the measurement. Measure the depth. Cut a piece of the velour paper to this measurement. Peel off the backing on one short edge. Lay the exposed sticky surface along the bin. Smooth the velour onto the bin, peeling the backing off gradually. Trim with braid and fringing.

Dressing table set

Materials required

Self-adhesive velour paper
Heavy cardboard
Braid and fringing, decorative edging
Gilt braid, acetate film
Adhesive tape
Fabric adhesive, clear all-purpose adhesive

Tools you will need

Sharp crafts' knife, scissors
Pair of pencil compasses
Ruler, pencil

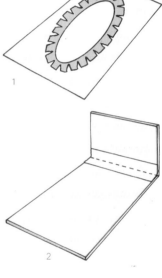

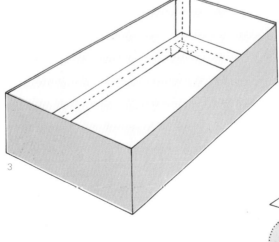

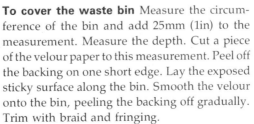

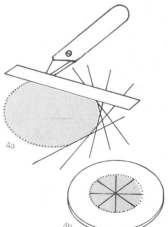

Papercrafts

Paper, in its different forms, is a most versatile medium. Tissue paper and crêpe paper, one crisp and thin, the other soft and stretchy, are used to make lovely artificial flowers. In this chapter, the techniques of papier mâché, flower making, and découpage are described.

Bouquet of summer flowers

A beautifully made bouquet of paper flowers is an unusual gift. Paper flowers cost very little to make and, once you have mastered the basic techniques, you will probably feel that you could invent some flower forms of your own. The rose shapes given here would also make peonies and the carnation shape could become a pink.

Making the paper patterns The diagram showing the flower petal and leaf shapes is to a scale of 1 square to 50mm (2in). If you can obtain squared paper to this scale, copy the shapes from the diagram on p.76. Alternatively, mark a sheet of tracing paper into 50mm (2in) squares. Do not worry if your drawn up shapes are not exactly as the diagram. The shapes are not critical and if your petals have an uneven outline, it will not matter. When you have made one or two flowers, you will be able to cut petals from the crêpe paper direct.

Giant rose To make a giant rose you will need red or pink crêpe paper, green for the calyx, stem and the leaves.

Cut 6 of the outer petals (1). Cut 6 inner petals (2). Cut the inner bud piece (3). Cut one calyx (4), and a number of leaves (5), from green paper. The leaves are cut with pinking shears and are used in pairs.

Cut a piece of the thick wire about 20cm (8in) long. Spread a little glue along the right hand edge of the bud piece and press the wire onto it. Roll up the bud and twist the stem part to the wire very tightly. Glue the six inner petals round the bud, each opposite another. Glue on the six outer petals. Glue the calyx under the outer petals last. Curl the edges of the outer petals by stretching them between the thumb and a pencil. Using both thumbs and forefingers, stretch the outer petals into a slight bowl shape. Tear a narrow strip from the green crêpe paper.

Wind it round the stem, starting under the calyx, using a little glue to hold it securely. Cut short pieces of the thin wire. Glue a piece of wire to a leaf shape, glue another leaf shape on top, sandwiching the wire. Cover the leaf stalk with wound paper strip and then bind the leaves to the main stem with more strips. Bend the leaves realistically.

Hollyhock For hollyhocks, use yellow, pink, dark red and white crêpe paper with green for the leaves.

Cut two strands of wire for the stem about 60cm (24in) long. Each stem will have three large flowers, two smaller flowers, two half-opened buds with centres, four buds without centres, four small buds and three very small buds.

Bind the two strands of wire together with strips of green paper.

Start with the small buds at the top of the stem. Make small balls of cotton wool and bind them in small squares of pale green crêpe paper, using the thin wire. Trim away some of the bunched paper under the ball. Twist the wire onto the stem. Bind green paper round.

Make larger buds, as you proceed down the stem, in the same way. Then make one or two buds which are just starting to open. Glue a small strip of a coloured paper across the top of the ball to show the petals just coming through.

The small flowers come next. Cut 6 frilled petals (6) and one calyx (7) for each flower. Bunch the petals round a piece of wire, add the calyx and then twist the wire round the stem. Bind with the green strip.

For the larger flowers, cut a fringed centre (8) in white, bunch it round a piece of wire and then add 12 frilled petals. Add 6 outer petals, (9), and then the calyx. Cover the wire with green paper and twist it on to the stem. Bind the stem. Now make three or four leaves (10).

Cut out leaves in pairs and glue two together, sandwiching a piece of thin wire between. Twist the wires to the stem and then bind the stem.

Carnation You will need pink and dark red crêpe paper with green for the leaves and stem.

Cut a fringed centre (11) and bunch it round a thin wire stem. Cut 12 petals (12) and cut the edge with pinking shears. Bunch round the centre and secure with thin wire. Wire the flower to the main stem and cover the flower stem and the main stem with strips of green

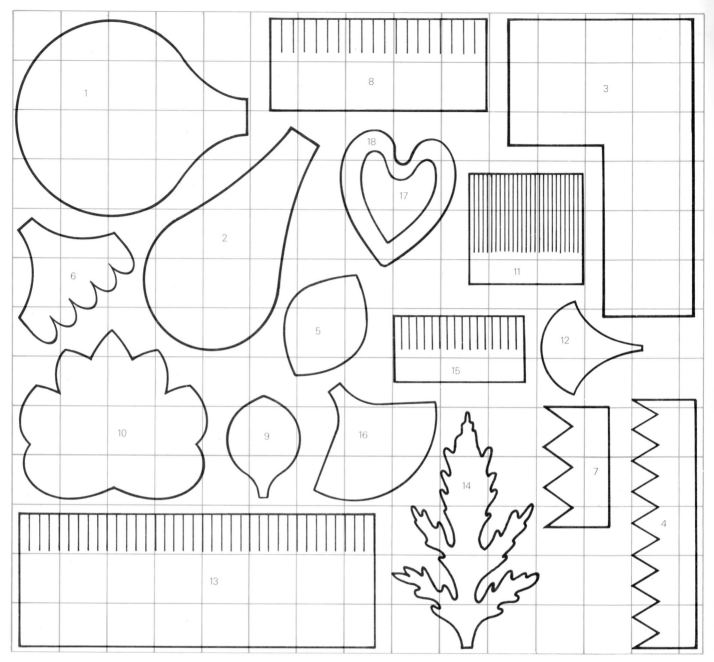

paper. Cut thin strips of green paper and glue them to strands of thin wire for leaves. Wire and then bind them to the stem. Make three or four flowers to a stem.

Giant Poppy You will need black, scarlet and green crêpe paper.

Wrap a square of black paper round a ball of cotton wool, on a piece of thick wire for a stem. Twist and glue the paper under the ball round the stem.

Cut a fringe (13) in black and bunch it round the ball. Glue the fringe round the stem. Cut seven outer petals from the rose outer petals pattern (1). Glue the base of the petals only round the stem just under the ball. Do not wrap the petals round the ball.

Pull and crease the petals over a pencil. Stretch the petals between the thumbs and forefingers of both hands to make the petals bowl-shaped.

Cut leaves (14) in pairs, making them up as for rose leaves. Wire to the stem and bind the stem.

Morning Glories You will need, yellow, pale blue and green crêpe paper.

Cut a fringed centre in yellow (15) and glue it, bunched, round a 50mm (2in) stem of thin wire. Cut out the flower shape (16) in blue and glue the edges A and B together to make a trumpet shape round the yellow centre. Bind the stem with strips of green paper. Make several flowers.

Cut pairs of leaves in green (there are two sizes (17, 18)), and make up leaves with wire as for rose leaves. Bind flowers and leaves on doubled strands of thin wire. Pull the edges of the petals a little to flute them. Make tiny leaves of the same shape and glue to the tips of the strands.

Jewelled tree

Jewelled tree

Materials required

Medium-weight flexible wire
Gold-foil paper (or newspaper and gold paint)
Wallpaper paste
Food tub, Polyfilla
Gift wrap paper or poster paints and small amount toilet soap
Epoxy adhesive

Tools you will need

Wire cutters
Brush
Scissors, needle

The exquisite little tree is an ornament, hung with flowers made from beads. Using the same technique, a dressing table jewellery tree could be made, to hold rings, necklaces and bracelets.

The basic technique for making the tree is called 'armature making' and is a papier mâché technique, used by modellers when making figures.

To make the tree Cut 21 strands of wire, 45cm (18in) long. Twist the wires together in threes and then gently twist the 7 groups of three together to make the lower trunk. Twist three groups together and then two groups of three to make roots. Study the illustration and bend the tree to make a twisted trunk like a bonsai tree.

There are three main branches. Divide the 21 strands into groups of seven. Make smaller branches of two strands and one of three strands. Clip groups short and bend the branches naturally. Paste 12mm (½in) wide strips of gold-foil paper or newspaper and wind them around the branches. Tear narrower strips for the thinner branches. If you are using newspaper, leave the pasted paper to dry completely before painting it gold.

The leaves on the tree illustrated are small leaves taken from bought plastic flowers and painted gold. Alternatively, you could make leaves from gold paper, cutting two leaf shapes and glueing them back to back over a strand of wire. Mark the veins of the leaf with a needle point, pressing into the foil paper.

Wire the leaves to the tree branches in two's. Touch up the wire with gold paint.

If you are making a jewelled tree, glue beads together to make flower shapes using epoxy adhesive. Thread wire through the beads to attach them to the tree branches. If you are making a tree for holding jewellery, bend the tips of the branches up a little. Cover a food pot with a pretty gift paper or paint it with poster colours, mixed with a little toilet soap, to make the paint stick to the plastic surface.

Mix the Polyfilla powder with water to make a rough, thick consistency. Stand the tree in the pot and spoon the Polyfilla in around the roots. Leave to dry. Paint the surface of the Polyfilla with gold paint.

Attach the bead flowers to the branches, twisting the wire to hold them securely. Touch up the wire with gold paint.

The art of découpage

Découpage is an old craft and is supposed to have originated in Italy during the Renaissance. Chinese and Japanese handpainted furniture was being imported into Europe and the artisans of Florence, unable to imitate the exquisite hand painting, endeavoured to reproduce the effect by cutting out paper prints and glueing them to the furniture they were making. The prints were hand-coloured and then varnished. The effect was similar in appearance to the handpainted objet d'art, and a vogue began for the relatively inexpensive copies. The art of découpage — cutouts — spread to France and the ladies of the French court cut up many valuable and irreplaceable original engravings in the pursuit of the craft. Victorian ladies knew about découpage but, for some years, this pleasant and inexpensive handicraft has not been as popular.

Now that craftsmen are again looking to the old crafts, découpage is enjoying a revival.

What is découpage? Nowadays, découpage is a craft whereby prints and engravings are carefully cut out and then glued to a wooden or a painted background as a decoration. The prints can be coloured, or plain and hand coloured. After being glued down, clear vanish is applied until the print is buried beneath as many as 30 coats, in some instances. The print glows through the layers of varnish with a beautiful effect and looks very like careful hand painting.

Materials required

Scissors are the first and most important requirement. It pays to buy the very best that you can afford. Choose cuticle scissors because these have curved blades and are ideal for the job. The scissors should be about 75mm (3in) long, overall.

Prints Ideally, prints for découpage should be on thin paper because not only are these easier to cut out but fewer coats of varnish are needed to cover the paper edges. Studios and printers who specialize in selling découpage prints to craftsmen have reprints of engravings by master draughtsmen such as Jean Pillement, Watteau and Boucher. These prints are of flower garlands, Chinese figures, rustic scenes and so on and are the traditional decorative motifs for furniture.

However, suitable motifs for découpage can be obtained from other sources. Gift wrapping papers have a variety of designs, traditional and modern, and the paper is generally thin.

Wallpaper sample books can provide lovely designs and old books sometimes have line drawings and engravings which you can have photostatted and colour by hand.

Colour pencils are best for colouring — the varnish affects the colour less — and enthusiasts often say that colouring prints is much of the fun in decoupage. Pencils produce the delicacy of effect that is important in this charming craft.

Pastes and glues Only water-soluble pastes are suitable for decoupage. It is important that every scrap of glue should be removed from the surface of the print before the varnish is applied and water soluble glues are the easiest to remove. The excess glue can be removed with a dampened sponge. There are several brands of soluble glues on the market. They are usually white in colour.

Varnish Traditionally, a good quality clear, no-colour varnish was used for découpage. Modern polyurethane gloss varnishes have the advantage that they dry very quickly. Some have a yellowish tinge to them which makes a white background look quite yellow after a few coats. Clear, no-colour varnish, specially pre-

pared for découpage, can be obtained from specialist craft shops.

Brushes Without doubt, buy the best you can obtain. They will last for years if you take care of them and the investment is worthwhile. If you choose a cheap brush it will frequently shed hairs and nothing is more annoying than to have a bristle drop out and stick itself to a beautiful piece of découpage.

Other equipment You will also need fine sandpaper, steel wool, a small sponge, warm water, blotting paper, solvent in a jar for cleaning the varnish brush, a sharp crafts' knife and some lintless cloth.

How to do découpage

Preparing the surface The surface of the item must be smooth. It can be made of wood or metal but every projection and unevenness must be sanded down or filled in. Rub down the surface with fine sandpaper and then with steel wool. The surface is then ready for painting or staining.

Painting Water paints or oil paints can be used for découpage but remember, if you are painting the item white, most varnishes will turn the white yellow. Pale blue takes on a greenish tinge.

Cutting out A famous découpage expert once said that cutting out was the most important stage in the craft. Actually, it is a most enjoyable and absorbing occupation. With a sharp pair of scissors and a little practice, you will become expert at cutting out quite intricate shapes. Some découpagists use transfers for their pieces but nothing can compare with a hand cut print, beautifully mounted and varnished. The technique for cutting out is simple: hold the print in your left (or non-working) hand. Hold the scissors in the other hand with the points curving away from you. Now move the paper through the blades, opening and closing them smoothly. The hand holding the scissors does not move at all. The paper is fed into the blades with the left hand, the hand turning and curving to present the lines of the print to the blades. The cut edge should have a slightly 'feathered' look because this makes pasting down far easier.

When cutting inside corners, make sure that they are sharp and clean. The outline of the design can be cut first or you can begin to cut from inside the design. It really does not matter and enthusiasts follow both methods. Leave thin strips of paper between delicate areas — these are called 'bridges' and these will hold the design together. The bridges can be cut away with a blade after the print is pasted down.

Pasting The adhesive can be applied in either of two ways. You can smear adhesive all over the painted surface and then lay the cutout print down on it. Or, you can brush the adhesive on to the back of the print, spreading it to the edges.

Découpagists follow both methods and either will do as long as the print is properly stuck down. Press any air bubbles under the surface to the edges with the finger tips. If large bubbles persist, you may have to slit the print with a blade and press the air and adhesive out. After all the bubbles have been removed, wipe away any glue on the surface with a scrap of cotton wool dipped in water. Blot up any moisture left behind with blotting paper. Leave the print to dry.

Varnishing The varnishing stage may seem the easiest but in fact, it takes a lot of patience and is the time when a good piece of work can be spoiled through rushing. Take your time over varnishing and you will always be rewarded with perfect work.

Spray the pasted down print first with artist's fixative. Leave it to dry and then wipe with a lintless cloth. Now dip just the bristles of your brush in the varnish and apply your first coat of varnish.

Apply the varnish with long strokes. Lift the brush at the end of each stroke. Brush off as much as you can leaving just a thin film. Leave the piece to dry in a dustfree place.

In most homes, there is always dust in the air and, no matter how careful you are, dust will settle on your newly applied coat of varnish.

You can avoid this happening by making yourself a tent of polythene sheeting and putting the piece underneath to dry. Otherwise, prepare a large cardboard box and stand the piece in the box. It is at least protected from lint floating through the air.

Ten coats of varnish are applied and each is left to dry out thoroughly. After the tenth coat, the edges of the print should have been covered and you will not be able to feel them through the varnish. At this stage, sanding down begins. Wrap a piece of fine sandpaper around a matchbox and rub all over the varnished surface in a circular motion. Wash the surface clean and wipe dry. Rub down with steel wool. Rub clean again and you are ready for the next coat of varnish. From now, apply a coat of varnish and rub down between coats. When about 30 coats have been applied, give a final polish with a good wax polish.

What can be découpaged?

Old wooden boxes, trays, small tables, chests, chairs and so on, can be worked. Some people decoupage tin and other metal objects. Glass takes prints well.

Stick prints inside glass bowls or bottles and paint the surround. The effect is rather like fine porcelain. Glass plates make effective wall plaques. Glue a fruit or flower print to the wrong side of a clear glass plate. Paint the background round the print an opaque colour. Varnish the paint and print afterwards.

Papier mâché

The art of papier mâché was invented in Paris during the reign of Louis XIV. There were many rival theatre companies in the city, all vying with each other for the custom of the playgoers. Programmes were changed frequently and, all over Paris, posters were being put up, one over another. Soon, a thick wad of paper and glue built up and thrifty Parisians saw a use for the material. The wads were prised from the walls, cut into pieces, soaked in water and shaped to make trinket boxes which were decorated and sold. Eventually, a British business man copied the technique and made papier mâché himself which he had shaped into coach panels. Later still, another business man called Henry Clay developed the craft still further and made all kinds of 'paperware' which was made from layers of paper pasted together, oiled, varnished and baked in ovens. By the time of the Great Exhibition in London in 1851, all kinds of papier mâché furnishings were being made. However, the craze died out at the end of the 19th century and examples of papier mâché furniture can now be seen only in museums. Papier mâché is reviving as a craft because it is inexpensive — only paper and paste are involved — and because people are looking for ways of re-using raw materials wherever they can. Newspaper makes the best papier mâché — and what could be cheaper?

Two techniques

There are two techniques in papier mâché. One uses pulped paper which is moulded and shaped in much the same way as clay. The other is called the layering technique. Sometimes, the two techniques are combined in a project.

Layering is worked in two ways. For finely shaped or delicate pieces, small squares of paper are pasted over a mould. For larger items, whole sheets of old newspaper are pasted over a suitable mould.

Method 1 — piece layering Mix up some wallpaper paste. (You can use flour and water paste if you prefer.) Tear newspaper into pieces, small squares about 25mm (1in) or pieces 50mm × 25mm (2in × 1in) depending on the shape of the pieces you are working on. Prepare the mould by covering the surface with oil. Dip pieces of paper in the paste, removing the excess between the forefinger and thumb of the other hand. Lay pieces all over the surface of the mould, crisscrossing pieces and overlapping edges. After putting on two layers, allow the paper to dry out before applying more layers. Depending on the piece being made, 5-10 layers are applied.

Method 2 — sheet layering This method is most suitable for working on a flat surface such as a tray. Oil the tray all over the top surface. Use large pages of newspaper. Paste the first sheet on both sides and smooth onto the tray. Paste the next sheet on one side only and smooth over the tray. Do not trim the edges at this stage. Paste down three or four layers and leave to dry.

The next day, the paper will be like leather and not quite dried out. Cut the extra paper off using scissors. Smooth the edge with a little paste. Apply two more layers of paper and leave to dry. When at the leather stage, cut off the excess paper and apply two more layers. Trim and then add the final two layers, nine in all. When the paper has completely dried out, prise the shape from the tray. Turn the tray over, oil it and layer the underside of the tray in the same way. When both layers are finished and dried, lay them together and join the edges with strips of pasted paper. To obtain a good finish for painting, you can either cover the whole surface with tiny scraps of white tissue paper, pasting it down in 25mm (1in) squares, or you can paint the surface with two or three coats of white emulsion paint, sanding the surface smooth with fine sandpaper afterwards.

Things to make in papier mâché

Projects using moulds All kinds of things can be used for moulds and covered with paper using the piece layering technique. Bowls and dishes can be reproduced to make gaily painted party dishes. Bottles and jars can be used for moulds too. Oil the outside surface and cover with five or six layers. Cut the papier mâché from the mould using a sharp crafts' knife. Cut down both sides and across the bottom and take the bottle or jar out. Paste the two halves back together with pasted paper strips.

Balls and balloons can be used to make hollow spheres. Blow up the balloons and oil the surface. Rest the balloon on a basin and layer the surface. Hollow spheres will make animal shapes, such as a savings pig. Half spheres will make party masks.

Papier mâché can also be worked leaving the mould in position under the layers. Toy shapes can be worked on discarded plastic containers and bottles. An animal can be made on a liquid detergent bottle using four corks for legs.

Pretty candlesticks for table decorations can be made from three or four glass jars. Glue the jars, one on top of another, with pieces of thick card in between. Cover the surface with paper strips. Paint with enamel colours. The top jar holds the candle.

Ordinary cardboard boxes can be taped together to make simple shelf units and covered with 10-12 layers of newspaper, torn into 10cm (4in) squares.

Plant pot cover

Materials required

Flower pot, earthenware or plastic
Plastic sheeting (food bag would do)
Adhesive tape
Newspaper, torn into squares and strips
Wallpaper paste, oil
Gesso powder, white emulsion paint for undercoat
Enamel paints for decoration, transfers, paper cutouts etc.
Polyurethane varnish

Tools you will need

Jar or bottle
Brushes for paste, paint and varnish
Scissors
Fine sandpaper

Plant pot cover (far right) and Savings pig. See instructions on page 94 for making the Savings pig.

Plant pot cover

Ceramic plant pot covers are expensive to buy but you can make a very pretty cover for a flower pot in papier mâché. The finished cover is given two or three coats of polyurethane varnish to make it durable.

To prepare the cover The cover for the flower pot must be slightly larger. To make the mould larger therefore, tear strips of newspaper and wind them round the pot. Secure them with tape. Pad the flower pot at least 9mm (³/₁₆in) with paper strips. Slip the padded pot into a piece of plastic sheeting or into a food bag and tape the plastic to fit the pot closely. Oil the plastic.

Stand the pot on a jar or bottle upside down and start applying pasted paper pieces. Apply two layers and leave to dry. Apply two more layers and leave to dry. Continue until you have built up 10 layers.

Remove the paper shape from the mould and pull out the plastic sheet and padding. Trim the top edge of the pot cover with scissors. Mix gesso powder with water to a thick paste and paint all over the pot inside and outside. Leave to dry and then apply a second layer. This makes the surface smooth for painting.

Painting and finishing Give the pot two coats of undercoat and then sand the surface with fine sandpaper to make it smooth, if it needs it.

Decorating your pot cover You can simply paint the papier mâché pot cover with gloss enamel paint and leave it at that. Many people like plain coloured pot covers.

If you have the skill to paint a design, keep motifs simple and use modeller's enamel paints. You could stencil a design on one side, (see page 42 for stencilling techniques), or you can decorate the pot with paper cutouts using the découpage techniques described on pages 78-79. Flowers cut from gardener's catalogues or from wallpaper would make pretty motifs for a plant pot. Or, you can use decal transfers.

String and card appliqué This is a fascinating decorative technique and makes the finished pot look as though it were made of painted clay. Cut shapes from cardboard, circles, squares, diamonds, hearts etc. (You could trace round small pastry cutters for shapes.)

Cut out the shapes. Glue them to the sides of the pot cover. Cut short lengths of thick, smooth string. Glue the string to the pot, making waving lines and spirals. Leave everything to dry thoroughly. Paint all over the appliquéd shapes. When the paint is dry, pick out the shapes and string in contrast colours or simply in a single contrast colour.

Tissue paper painting Paint the pot in a light, single colour, white, pale yellow or pink. Cut petal shapes from tissue paper. Smear paste on the pot surface and lay down the petal shapes, overlapping them. Use toning colours, such as pinks, reds, oranges etc., for natural looking effects. Cut out green leaf shapes. Arrange groups of petals to make flowers with leaves around them. Draw stems if you like with felt-tipped pens. Leave everything to dry and then apply two or three thin coats of clear varnish.

Finishing The undercoating and coats of enamel paint will make the plant pot cover waterproof but, to keep the decoration from getting damaged or worn, give the finished pot two or three coats of clear, polyurethane varnish, whatever method of decoration you use. Varnish the inside of the pot too.

Handmade cards

Making your own greetings cards is enjoyable as well as being much cheaper — one sheet of good quality card will make up to a dozen greetings cards. But, think how pleasant it is to receive a card which not only looks quite different from any other, but has obviously been made with a special occasion in mind.

The ideas here involve a number of different techniques. Do not worry if you cannot draw or paint. Very few of the cards illustrated involve actual drawing.

Materials required

Papers and cards Greetings cards are meant to stand up without flopping over or curling. Choose a really good quality card or paper and your finished cards will look professional. This is one area where you should not economize. Thin, rigid card in white and a few pastel colours can be bought at art shops. Construction paper or cartridge paper is made in a wide range of colours and can be bought at most large stationers and art shops.

Cutting tools The most important piece of equipment you need is something to cut with. The best tool is a crafts' knife with interchangeable blades. These are safe to use. Alternatively, a one-sided razor blade knife (the blade is fixed into a safety holder) is almost as good. You will also need something to cut on — a piece of hardboard is ideal — and a metal ruler.

A pair of scissors will be needed for some jobs. Have a pair about 15cm (6in) long. Do not use the scissors from the workbasket because cutting paper will blunt the blades.

You also need a set square for making square corners, some felt tipped pens, paint brushes, drawing pens, drawing ink, poster paints and coloured inks, pencils and so on, depending on the technique you are using.

Glues and adhesives Glues should be the type which dry quickly and without making a stain or showing too much. PVA adhesives which are white in colour are good. This type of adhesive comes in bottles and applicators and also in a 'glue pen' which puts down tiny spots of glue.

These are particularly good for collage jobs. Glues in stick form, rather like a lipstick, are extremely good for sticking down paper on paper and are easy for children to use. Clear, quick-drying adhesives are used for collage or when heavy items are being stuck down. Rubber solution works well but leaves a smell behind. Latex-based adhesives are good for sticking down fabrics and yarns.

Preparing the basic card Before deciding on the size of the greetings card, look at the range of sizes of envelopes available at a stationers. Postal authorities dislike odd shapes and sizes in envelopes because postal sorting is automated in many places and oddly sized cards and envelopes cannot be handled easily. Try and work to an envelope size which already exists, even if you are going to make your own envelopes.

Draw out the size on the paper you are using, using the edges of the paper as a starting point. Remember that if the fold of the card is going to be on the left, the front of the card is on the right Mark in the fold very lightly in pencil. Use your set square to make sure that all the corners are square before cutting out. If the design you are planning is going to run off the sides of the card, cut the card out after finishing the design. To cut out, lay the metal ruler along the pencilled line, so that the waste paper is to your right. Draw the tip of the knife blade along the line gently. Make two or three cuts to cut through the paper if necessary. Do not try and do it in one cut.

Making a sharp fold No matter what type of design you do, the fold of the greetings card must be clean and sharp if it is going to look professional. To achieve this, a fold must be scored first. Here is how it is done. Hold the ruler along the lightly pencilled fold line. With the tip of the knife blade, cut lightly along the line so that you cut just about halfway through the thickness of the paper. The paper or cardboard will now fold easily along the scored line. Fold along the line and then press the fold with your thumbnail.

Mounting on a greetings card Sometimes you will do your design directly onto the card and at other times, the design will be worked out on a separate piece of paper and mounted on the greetings card afterwards. When mounting, dot the glue in the corners of the paper and along the sides if it is very large, then press it down on the greetings card. Never spread glue all over the back because it will not go down smoothly and will spoil the finished effect.

Folds and shapes Cards can either have a single fold or can be folded twice from a square of paper. Or, you can make concertina folds, folding first one way and then the other. If you are making a card with a decorative outline, make sure that the fold is left intact when you cut out (*diagram 1*).

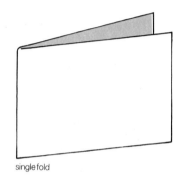

single fold

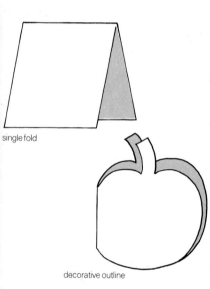

single fold

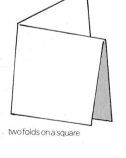

decorative outline

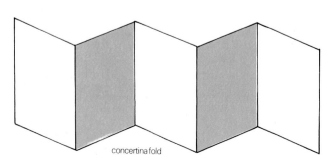

two folds on a square

concertina fold

1

Design ideas

Here are some ideas and techniques for making greetings cards. Not all of them are illustrated and they are intended to set you thinking rather than give you patterns to copy.

Collage

☐ PAPER COLLAGE Whenever you get a gift wrapped in gift paper, keep a piece for making greetings cards. Sometimes there will be a complete motif which you can cut out and mount on a coloured background. Or, there may be an area of pattern which can be cut out in geometric shapes and put together again.

Colour magazines will provide you with large areas of colour. Once a shape is cut from a colour photograph, it provides just colour and the content of the picture no longer 'reads'. Cut out simple shapes and add shapes cut from plain coloured paper to make designs.

Lacy paper doyleys make pretty cards for birthdays or anniversaries. Trim lacy edges away and outline a design or use just the centre of a doyley, mounted on a bright or dark coloured paper.

☐ TISSUE PAPER COLLAGE Try tearing scraps of coloured tissue paper into shapes and pasting them down to make an abstract design. The transparent tissue looks rather like watercolour painting. Or cut shapes with scissors to make up designs. You might like to try cutting rose petals in two or three different pinks, mounting them into a flower, overlapping the edges. Draw in a stem afterwards in black ink.

☐ DRIED FLOWERS COLLAGE Preserve some flowers and leaves (see page 32) and keep them for making gift cards and greetings cards all through the year. Stick the petals and leaves down with just a touch of glue and to protect the surface afterwards, cover the card with a sheet of adhesive, transparent film.

☐ FELT AND FABRIC COLLAGE Felt is a lovely material for making collage pictures. Add sequins, small buttons, pieces of lace, scraps of ribbon and so on to make a card which will be treasured and kept. Try making a lace trimmed card, like the one illustrated. This is a St Valentines card but you could make birthday cards and anniversary cards using lace edging in the same way. Cut a piece of bright felt for the background. Cut out a heart shape in a plain or patterned fabric. Glue the heart down onto the felt, pushing a piece of cotton wool underneath for padding. Sew lace round the heart. Add a bow if you like. Glue the felt to a card made of fairly stiff paper or card. Write a message inside.

☐ WOOL COLLAGE Work out a simple design. Cut lengths of coloured wool. Spread glue thinly on the design, working one area at a time. Lay the lengths of wool on the background, pushing it with a matchstick or a knitting needle so that it follows the lines of the design. Fill in some areas with wool, working it round and round inside the shape. Leave other areas simply outlined.

Cut-out shapes Some of the motifs on pages 40-41 can be used to make greetings cards. Use them full size or enlarge them by copying them on squared paper. Trace the shapes down onto folded paper or card. One edge of the design should be against the fold. Cut out the shape, making sure that you keep some of the fold intact.

Stained glass windows This technique makes a very pretty Christmas card. Work out a simple design on paper and draw another line 3mm (⅛in) away from the design lines so that you have a doubled line. Join all the lines up (*diagram 2*). Trace the design down onto black paper (use chalk on the back of your tracing to transfer the lines). With a sharply pointed blade, cut out the spaces between the design lines. Save some sweet wrappings made of coloured transparent film. Glue pieces behind the cutout design. Mount the stained glass window on a card made of stiff, thin white paper. When the card is stood near to a lamp or a window, the colours will glow, rather like a church window.

Lettering messages The hardest part of making your own gift card is getting a professional effect with the words. For most cards, it is better to keep the design on the front entirely graphic and not have any words at all. Then you can write the message on the inside of the card. For some types of cards, the message is the most important part — such as a congratulatory card or an announcement about a new baby. You can work out the lettering in either of two ways. For an amusing card, cut letters from magazines or newspapers and paste them down, making words and sentences. Alternatively, use the rub down letters which can now be bought at most stationers. You can choose small capital letters for long messages or a large, decorative initial letter to make a name or a word.

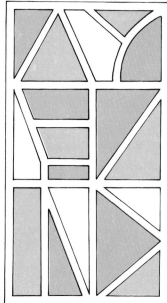

2

83

All wrapped up

Wrapping presents is as much a skill as making them and adds the finishing touch to your gift. You can achieve lovely effects quite simply through the careful choice of paper and ribbon.

Pages from colour magazines, if carefully selected, make a very interesting and smart-looking gift wrap paper. The secret is to choose a picture where the colour is massed in large areas and then choose a ribbon to match the strongest colour.

Boxes

Wrapping a square or rectangular box Make sure that you have enough gift wrap paper. If necessary, tape two sheets together first. Use a glue stick for sealing edges. Transparent adhesive tape always shows and looks rather messy.

Lay the box on the paper. Bring up the sides and then trim the overlap to about 50mm (2in). Fold the edge of the overlap under. The paper should extend over the ends a little more than half the depth of the box. Glue the overlap down. Fold the sides in first and then the top flap down and the bottom flap up. Glue or fasten with a doubled piece of transparent tape, placed under the flaps so that it does not show.

Wrapping round boxes Trace the bottom and top of the box on the wrong side of the paper. Cut out two circles. Measure the length of the box and the circumference. Cut a piece of paper with 25mm (1in) extra at both ends and with 25mm (1in) extra on the length for the overlap. Roll the paper round the box. Fold under the edge of the overlap. Glue it down. Snip into the extra paper at the ends of the box to make tabs. Fold them in. Spread a little glue round the edges of the two circles of paper and press them onto the cut tabs.

For long tubes, wrap a lightweight paper, such as tissue, round the tube with about 50mm (2in) overlapping the ends. Tie round the ends and then fringe the overlaps with scissors so that the parcel looks like a cracker. Wrap a strip of foil paper round the tube to complete the effect.

Ribbons and bows

Diagram 1 shows some of the ways in which decorative adhesive tape can be used on different box shapes. If you use an adhesive tape in this way, you can add a bow or a rosette made from ribbon. Flowers, made of coloured tissue paper (see page 74), make very pretty gift wrap decorations.

Chrysanthemum Cut 40cm (16in) lengths of gift ribbon down the middle of the strips. Moisten the ends and join them. Turn the loop into a

figure-of-eight shape and moisten to hold the shape. Join two figure-of-eights, using a touch of glue (*diagram 2*). Add more loops, laying them first one way, then the other, until you have made a chrysanthemum. You will need about 15 loops to achieve the effect.

Daisy Cut 4 pieces of gift ribbon, 20cm (8in) long. Lay the pieces, one on another to make a star shape (*diagram 3*), glueing them at the centre. Bring the ends up and fasten together. Spread a little glue, or moisten the surface of the inside of the ball shape at top and bottom. Push the top and bottom together and hold until they stick together.

Petal Moisten the end of a strip of gift ribbon and make a small ring. Wind the ribbon round, moisten the surface and make another, slightly larger ring (*diagram 4*). Continue in the same way until you have made a petal shape. Use petal shapes flat to make a flower, or fasten several together in a heap, by the long ends. Ribbon petals can also be made to look like butterfly shapes. Glue four together, two on each side of a ribbon body.

Easy bow You can make this of self-adhesive gift ribbon or from real ribbon. Cut a strip of ribbon and join both ends to the middle. Cut a short strip and bind it over the middle, joining the ends on the underside of the bow.

Make a bigger bow by cutting a long strip of ribbon and glueing down a loop at one end. Make a loop at the other end, fastening at the centre. Continue to make loops at each end, each slightly shorter than the one before. Three or four loops at each end is sufficient. Cut a short strip and bind the centre (*diagram 5*).

Rosette bow You need narrow satin ribbon to make this. Loop the ribbon (*diagram 6*). Tie in the middle with another piece of ribbon. Fishtail-cut the ends of the tie. Spread out the loops.

Decorating with cutouts Attractive-looking gift wraps can be made without using ribbons at all. Fasten parcels with touches of glue or use adhesive tape, doubled on the underside of overlaps so that it does not show. Cut motifs from other gift papers or cut shapes from a contrasting paper. Glue to the outside of the wrapped parcel.

Creative gift wrapping

You can get very pretty effects with just gift wrap paper and ribbons but for really original wraps, you have to treat every wrapping job as an artist treats his canvas. Think about the things you can use as decoration, other than ribbons and bows. You can use glass balls for Christmas parcels, tying them in with the ribbons. You can cut poinsettia flowers from red paper, wiring them together by the stems. You can use preserved flowers to make posies for summer birthday parcels. Dried leaves can be

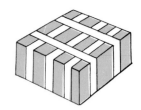
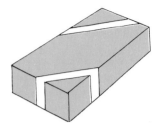
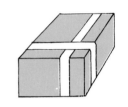

1

glued to a brown or cream-coloured paper. Letters can be outlined in glue and then sparkle dust sprinkled onto the wet glue. For children, you might thread soft, jelly sweets on strong thread and tie loops of sweets across a parcel. You can add a second gift as part of the gift wrapping. A sew-on picture patch — the kind that are used for decorating jeans — could be used as a gift tag for a young person's gift.

Naming gifts Names and initials can be made part of a parcel's decoration. Here are one or two ways to use letters. Cut big letters from newspapers or from posters. Glue them onto foil-wrapped parcels. Draw letters on the back of foil paper, as big as the top of the gift box. Glue them on a patterned paper. Draw a name or initial in glue. Lay thick yarn or ribbon along the wet glue to spell out a name.

Using rub-down letters, spell a name, putting each letter onto a gummed-back paper shape. Glue the shapes to the ends of ribbons. Glue one end of the ribbons to the top of the wrapped box, so that the letters spell out a name across the top.

Fabrics and yarns Try the effect of wrapping a box in fabric rather than paper. Use remnants of spot prints or gingham. Tie the boxes with real ribbon or sew the seams with thick, wool yarn. Use wool yarn as a tie.

Like something else By using coloured papers cleverly, you can make a wrapped parcel look like something else. A present for a child, packed in a square box, could be made to look

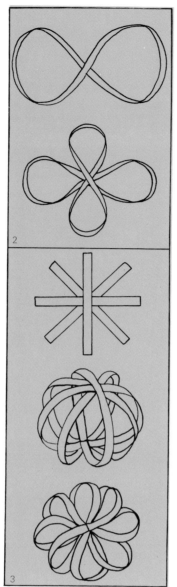

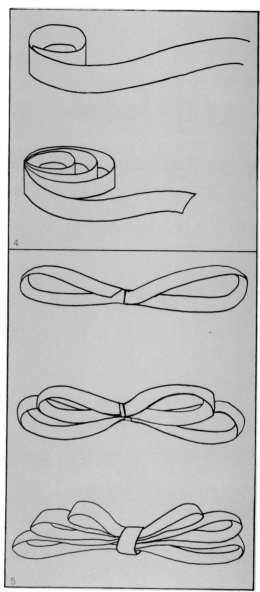

like a small house by cutting windows and door from coloured papers. Or a truck or train effect can be achieved with big wheels pasted on the box sides and windows cut from a foil paper.

Other kinds of containers For Christmas gifts, make a stocking shape in felt or in a strong paper. Decorate it with cutout shapes, flowers, Christmas motifs or letters.

Empty food pots, such as those used for cream, yoghurt or cream cheese can be turned into gift pots. Paint them in a bright colour, or gold. Cut a circle of gift paper with pinking shears. Push the paper into the pot, put in the gift, and draw the top closed with ribbon.

For Easter gifts, make your own paper eggs in papier mâché. See page 80 for the basic technique. An orange or a grapefruit used for a mould, makes a small gift egg. Use a melon or an inflated balloon for a larger egg. After the paper and paste have dried, cut the egg from the mould in two halves. Smooth off the cut edges. Paint the egg inside and out. Put in the gift and tie the halves together with ribbon.

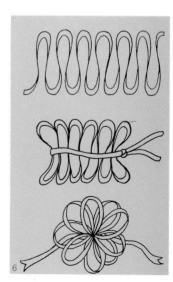

Knitting and crochet

Lacy wool shawl

This beautiful shawl would make a perfect family heirloom. The centre pattern with its dainty flower motif is gossamer-fine and the fringe makes the shawl look graceful. The shawl is made of a nylon yarn that is soft to the touch and yet wears and washes well.

To make the shawl

Using No. 2.50mm hook, make 288 ch loosely, turn.

Foundation row 1 dc in 2nd ch from hook, *1 dc in next ch, 4 ch, miss 3 ch, 1 tr in each of next 4 ch, 4 ch, miss 3 ch, 1 dc in each of next 2 ch. Rep from * to end.

1st row 1 ch, 1 dc in 1st dc, *4 ch, 2 tr in next 4 ch sp, 1 tr in next tr, 8 ch, miss 2 tr, 1 tr in next tr, 2 tr in next 4 ch sp, 4 ch, miss 1 dc, 1 dc in next dc. Rep from * to end.

2nd row 6 ch, *2 tr in next 4 ch sp, 1 tr in next tr, 4 ch, 1 dc in next 8 ch sp, 4 ch, miss 2 tr, 1 tr in next tr, 2 tr in next 4 ch sp, 2 ch. Rep from * ending last rep 2 tr in last 4 ch sp, 1 ch, 1 d tr in last dc.

3rd row 3 ch, 1 tr in 1 ch sp, *1 tr in next tr, 4 ch, 1 dc in next 4 ch sp, 1 dc in next dc, 1 dc in next 4 ch sp, 4 ch, miss 2 tr, 1 tr in next tr, 2 tr in next 2 ch sp. Rep from * ending last rep 1 tr in last tr, 1 tr in last ch sp, 1 tr in 5th of 6 ch.

4th row 9 ch, miss next tr, *1 tr in next tr, 2 tr in next 4 ch sp, 4 ch, miss 1 dc, 1 dc in next dc, 4 ch, 2 tr in next 4 ch sp, 1 tr in next tr, 8 ch, miss 2 tr. Rep from * but at end of last rep omit 8 ch and work 4 ch instead then miss 2 tr, 1 d tr into top of 3 ch.

5th row 1 ch, 1 dc in first d tr, *4 ch, miss 2 tr, 1 tr in next tr, 2 tr in next 4 ch sp, 2 ch, 2 tr in next 4 ch sp, 1 tr in next tr, 4 ch, 1 dc in next 8 ch sp. Rep from * ending last rep 1 dc in 4th of 9 ch instead of into 8 ch.

6th row 1 ch, 1 dc in 1st dc, *1 dc in next 4 ch sp, 4 ch, miss 2 tr, 1 tr in next tr, 2 tr in next 2 ch sp, 1 tr in next tr, 4 ch, 1 dc in next 4 ch sp, 1 dc in next dc. Rep from * to end.

The last 6 rows form patt. Cont. straight until work measures about 90cm (36ins) ending after a 3rd patt row, turn. Now work in rounds thus:

Next round 1 ch, 2 dc in 1st tr [place a marker in first of these 2 dc].
*1 dc in each of next 2 tr, 3 dc in next 4 ch sp, 1 dc in each of next 3 dc, 3 dc in next 4 ch sp, 1 dc in each of next 2 tr. Rep from * ending last rep 4 dc in 4 ch sp, instead of 3, then 1 dc in each of next 2 tr, 3 dc in top of 3 ch [place a marker in 2nd of last 3 dc], now work in dc down 1st side edge making sure that the number of dc along this edge, including last marked st, is a multiple of 5, plus an extra 4 sts, now work 3 dc in first ch of original ch [place a marker in 2nd of last 3 dc], work 287 dc evenly along lower edge [thus working 1 dc into each ch of foundation], and working 3 dc in the last ch [place a marker in 2nd of last 3 dc], now work in dc up 2nd side edge to match corresponding edge, then work 1 dc in the first st worked into, sl st in first marked st [note that there should be a multiple of 5, plus 4 extra sts in between each set of marked sts].

Work border thus:

1st round 1 ch, [1 dc, 7 ch, 1 dc] in first marked dc, [*7 ch, miss 4 dc, 1 dc in next dc. Rep from * to next corner, thus ending with 1 dc in next marked dc, 7 ch, 1 dc in same marked dc] 3 times, **7 ch, miss 4 dc, 1 dc in next dc. Rep from ** ending last rep, 3 ch, 1 d tr in first dc.

2nd round 1 ch, 1 dc in top of d tr, *7 ch, 1 dc in next 7 ch sp. Rep from * ending last rep 3 ch, 1 d tr in first dc.

3rd round As 2nd round.

4th round As 2nd round, but working [1 dc, 7 ch, 1 dc] into each of the 4 corner 7 ch sp.

Rep last 3 rounds once more, then 2nd and 3rd rounds again.

Fasten off.

Block shawl out with pins and press lightly using a cool iron and dry cloth. Cut remaining yarn into 225mm (9in) lengths and taking 5 strands together each time, knot all round edge in each 7 ch sp to form a fringe. Trim fringe.

Lacy wool shawl

Materials required

13 20gr balls Patons Baby 2-ply

Tools you will need

No. 2.50mm crochet hook
Scissors, pins

Measurements

Approximately 90cm (36in) square without border and fringe.

Tension

4 patterns measure about 162mm (6½in)

Abbreviations

ch chain
dc double crochet
tr treble crochet
d tr double treble
sp space
rep repeat
sts stitches
sl st slip stitch

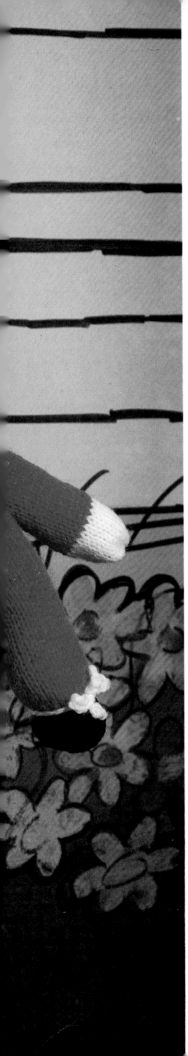

Sweet Sue

Sweet Sue is made on a candy tin. Fill the can with homemade sweets for a charming gift and when the sweets have been eaten, the doll still makes a shelf toy.

To make Sweet Sue
Body
With knitting needles and Red, cast on 60 sts.
1st row K.
2nd row K1. P to last st. K1.
Repeat last 2 rows 5 times.
Change to White and work rows 1 and 2.
Change to Red and work rows 1 and 2.
Rep last 4 rows twice more.
Change to White and work 26 rows in st.st. as before.
Cast off.

Arms
With knitting needles and Red, cast on 24 sts. Work 24 rows in st.st.
Change to White and work 10 rows in st.st. Do not cast off but run yarn through the stitches on needles and draw up tightly.

Legs
With knitting needles and Red, cast on 30 sts. Work in st.st. for 40 rows. Change to Black and work 6 rows in st.st.
Next row *K2 tog. Rep from * to end.
Next row K1. P to last st. K1.
Next row *K2 tog. Rep from * to last st. K1.
Next row K1. P to last st. K1.
Do not cast off. Thread yarn through all stitches and draw up tightly.

To make up
Sew up back seam of body section. Mark desired position of arms and legs. Stuff arms and legs and sew to body. Cut eyes and mouth from felt and sew onto White part of the body.

Hair
With crochet hook and Yellow, make 4ch., sl st to last ch. to form ring.
Work 8dc into ring, sl st to last dc.
1st round *2 lp sts into next dc. Rep from * all round. (16 sts.)
2nd round *1 lp st into next dc. 2 lp sts into next dc. Rep from * all round. (24 sts.)
Rep last round once more (36 sts.)
4th round 1 lp st into each dc all round. Rep 4th round until work measures about 14cm (5½in) from centre.
Fasten off.

Plaits Make 2 thick plaits with remainder of wool and stitch to underside of loop hair. Place the hair on top of the can. Make a bow and sew into the hair. Tie short strands of yarn round the doll's ankles.

Sweet Sue
Materials required

1 empty 1lb size coffee tin or can
2 25gr balls double knitting yarn, red
1 25gr ball double knitting yarn, white
3 25gr balls double knitting yarn, yellow
Small quantity of similar yarn, black
Scraps of felt for features
Kapok filling
Ribbon for bow

Tools you will need

2 No. 8 knitting needles
Crochet hook No. 5.50mm
Tape measure
Yarn needle
Scissors

Abbreviations

Knitting
K Knit
P Purl
Rep Repeat
Sts Stitches
St.st. Stocking stitch
Tog. Together

Crochet
ch chain
sl st slip stitch
dc double crochet
lp st loop stitch: work as follows: Insert hook into next dc, yarn over hook, draw up loop on index finger. Draw yarn through st, as in dc, yarn over hook and draw through loops on hook.

Knitted elephant

Knitted elephant

Materials required

Ten 25gr balls of washable Emu double knitting yarn
Felt or cotton materials for ears, eyes, soles etc.
Washable stuffing, sewing threads

Tools you will need

Pair of No. 10 knitting needles
Scissors
Needle, pins

Tension

7 sts. and 8 rows to 25mm (1in)

Measurements

Height: 23cm (9in); Length: 43cm (17in)

Abbreviations

sts. stitches
st.st. stocking stitch
K knit
P purl
tog. together
dec. decrease
cont. continue
inc. increase

Most knitters enjoy making toys. This pink elephant is made in stocking stitch in four shaped pieces. The toy illustrated has eyes and ears of felt. For a safe, washable toy, it would be better if they were made of cotton material.

To make the elephant

1st side

Cast on 8 sts. and work 2 rows st.st.
Cast on 5 sts. at beg. of next 4 rows.
☐ 7TH ROW Cast on 34 sts., k. to end.
☐ 8TH ROW P.
☐ 9TH ROW Cast on 3 sts. at beg. of row, k. to last st., k. twice into last st.
☐ 10TH ROW P. twice into first and last sts.
☐ 11TH ROW As 9th.
☐ 12TH ROW P. to last st., p. twice into last st.
Repeat last 4 rows once more.
☐ 17TH ROW K. twice into 1st and last st.
☐ 18TH ROW As 12th. Repeat last 2 rows twice more.
☐ 23RD ROW K. twice into 1st st., k. to end.
☐ 24TH ROW As 12th.
☐ 25TH ROW As 17th.
☐ 26TH ROW P.
☐ 27TH ROW As 23rd.
☐ 28TH ROW P.
Repeat last 4 rows once more.
☐ 33RD ROW As 17th.
☐ 34TH ROW P. twice into 1st st., p. to end.
☐ 35TH ROW K. to last st., k. twice into last st.
☐ 36TH ROW P. Repeat last 4 rows once more (109 sts.)
☐ 41ST ROW As 35th.
☐ 42ND ROW As 34th.
☐ 43RD ROW As 35th.
☐ 44TH ROW P.
☐ 45TH ROW K. 98, turn, leaving 14 sts. on spare needle. Work 3 rows st.st.
☐ 49TH ROW K. 80, cast off 3 sts., k. 8 turn. Leave last 7 sts. on needle.
☐ 50TH ROW Working on the 8 sts. p.2 tog. at each end of row.
☐ 51ST ROW K.2 tog. at each end of row. Cast off last 4 sts. Rejoin yarn at inner edge of the 7 sts. Cast off 2, k.5.
☐ NEXT ROW P.3, p.2 tog.
☐ NEXT ROW K.2 tog., k.2.
☐ NEXT ROW P.1, p.2 tog. Cast off last 2 sts. Rejoin yarn at inner edge of the 80 sts.
☐ NEXT ROW P.2 tog. p. to end.
☐ NEXT ROW K. Repeat last 2 rows 3 times more. (76 sts.) Work 13 rows st.st.*
☐ NEXT ROW K.50, k.2 tog., k. to end. Leave 50 sts. on a spare needle.
☐ NEXT ROW P. to last 2 sts., p.2 tog.

☐ NEXT ROW K.2 tog. k. to end. Repeat last 2 rows once more.
☐ NEXT ROW P. to last 2 sts., p.2 tog.
Work 16 rows st.st. Cast off last 20 sts.
With wrong side facing, rejoin yarn to inner edge of 50 sts. on spare needle. Cast off 25 sts. p. to end.
☐ NEXT ROW K. to last 2 sts., k.2 tog.
☐ NEXT ROW P.2 tog. p. to end. Repeat last 2 rows once more. K. to last 2 sts. k.2 tog. Work 16 rows st.st. Cast off last 20 sts.*
Rejoin yarn to inner edge of 14 sts. with right side facing.
☐ 1ST ROW Cast off 5, k. to last st., k. twice into last st.
☐ 2ND ROW Cast on 2 sts., p. to last 2 sts., p.2 tog.
☐ 3RD ROW Cast off 2 sts., k. to last st., k. twice into last st.
☐ 4TH ROW As 2nd.
Repeat last 2 rows 3 times more. Now dec. 1 st. at each end of next 4 rows.
☐ NEXT ROW K.2 tog. k.1. Cast off. Make another side to match reversing shaping.

Underside

Cast on 36 sts. Work 2 rows st.st. Cast on 10 sts. at beg. of next 4 rows. Work 8 rows st.st. Cont. as for first side from * to *.
Make another piece to match.

Rear section

Cast on 8 sts. Work 16 rows st.st.
☐ 17TH ROW K. twice into 1st st., k. to end.
☐ 18TH ROW P. to last st., p. twice into last st.
Repeat last 2 rows twice more. (14 sts.)
Cast on 14 sts. at beg. of next row. Do not knit across row. Break yarn. Now cast on 8 sts. on the same needle holding the 28 sts. Work 16 rows st.st. on 8 sts.
☐ 17TH ROW K. to last st., k. twice into last st.
☐ 18TH ROW P. twice into 1st st., p. to end.
Repeat last 2 rows twice more. (14 sts.) All 42 sts. should now be on the same needle, 2 legs with 14 cast on sts. in centre. Work 8 rows st.st.*
☐ NEXT ROW K.2 tog. at each end of row.
☐ NEXT ROW P. Repeat last 2 rows 3 times more. Take 2 tog. at each end of next 3 rows.
☐ NEXT ROW P. Repeat last 4 rows 3 times more. Take 2 tog. at each end of next 4 rows.
Cast off last 2 sts.

Chest

Work as for rear section from beg. to *.
Take 2 tog. at each end of next 3 rows.
☐ NEXT ROW P. Repeat last 4 rows 3 times more.
Take 2 tog. at each end of next row. Work 2 rows st.st. Repeat last 3 rows.
Take 2 tog. at each end of next row.
☐ NEXT ROW P. Work 20 rows st.st. Cast off last 12 sts.

Trunk under-section

Cast on 12 sts. and work 4 rows st.st.
☐ NEXT ROW K.2 tog. at each end. Work 5 rows st.st.

Repeat last 6 rows twice more. Inc. 1 st. into first st. of next 4 rows. Work 1 row. Cast off 10 sts.
To make up Press all pieces carefully. Join side sections together starting at trunk and ending approximately 125mm (5in) beyond cast on edge. Set rear section into back neatly. Set in trunk under-section and sew in chest section. Join the two under-sections, leaving 100mm (4in) open on straight edge for stuffing. Sew to sides of elephant, matching legs, etc.

Cut two ears in felt and sew to head. Make eyes from felt scraps and add to face. Cut 4 circles of felt and sew to bottom of feet and a small circle to end of trunk. Stuff firmly and close opening. Make a tail in plaited wool and attach to back. Add a felt flower to mouth.

To make a washable toy

Trace the shapes for eyes, ears, soles and trunk end. Use tracings for a pattern. Cut 4 ears, 4 feet soles, 1 trunk end, 2 eye-whites, 2 pupils in cotton fabric. Allow 6mm (¼in) seam allowance all round. Stitch 2 ear pieces together, wrong sides facing, to make 1 ear. Make 2 ears and stitch to elephant's head. Appliqué eye pupils to eyes, stitch to head. Sew soles to feet, turning in seam allowances.

Children only

This chapter is for you. Here are some ideas for gifts you can make for your mother and father, for uncles and aunts, for grandparents and friends.

Some of the things are very easy to make and are for younger children. Those on the next page are a little more difficult and are for older children. They do not cost very much to make but all of the gifts take time and trouble. And that is exactly what you should be giving when you make a present for someone, your time and your care. If you make the things just as carefully as you can, letting everything that is pasted or painted dry slowly and then, afterwards, wrapping your gift in a pretty paper or box, your gift is going to be the best kind of gift there is, made with love.

Mouse paperweight

The mouse is really a teasle and you can find these in the hedgerows or, perhaps, in the garden. Look for a big teasle, and cut the stem off short with sharp scissors. Now you need two whole cloves for eyes and one for the nose. See if there are any cloves in the kitchen jars that you could have. Otherwise, you could make eyes and nose from beads or from used matchstick heads. Glue the clove eyes and nose into the teasle. Next, look for a fircone. Pull off two of the

'leaves'. Glue them to the teasle mouse for ears. Cut two feet shapes from felt and glue them under the mouse body.

Last of all, you need a flat stone for the teasle mouse to sit on. Spread glue on the stone and rest the mouse on it. Leave it to dry.

Needlecases

Everyone who likes to sew, likes getting a needlecase. Mothers always look forward to getting a new one full of bright, new needles, especially when the case is amusing or pretty. The apple shape is a very easy shape to copy and so is the little house. You need some felt scraps, a needle and thread, some glue and a pair of scissors. If you can get hold of a pair of pinking shears, these are useful for cutting the inside pages neatly.

To make the apple, copy the apple shape from this page. You will need to draw the shape about

Now make the second rosette.

Iron your two rosettes and then snip out the basting stitches that held the papers in. They should just drop out when you shake the patchwork. Put the two rosettes together and right sides facing, oversew all round the sides. Leave one place open for putting in the stuffing. Turn inside out. Push in cotton wool with a pencil. When the pincushion is nice and full, finish sewing up the seam.

Spoon keyholder

Aren't you always hearing some grownup say 'where on earth have I put my keys?'. They never know where their keys are but if you make a keyholder and hang it in the kitchen or in the hall, perhaps they will remember to hang their keys on it and always know where they are.

This keyholder is just a wooden spoon with some hooks screwed into it and two rings for hanging the holder from a piece of ribbon.
Making the keyholder You need a fairly large wooden spoon. These can be bought from a kitchen shop and they are not very expensive. If the wood is rough, sand it smooth with a piece of sandpaper before painting it. Give the spoon an undercoat of white emulsion paint first. This will make the final painting much smarter. When it has dried, paint the spoon all over with a modeller's enamel paint. You can buy these tiny tins of paint quite cheaply and one tin is easily enough to paint a large spoon. Leave the spoon to dry for at least one whole day.

Next, make three holes in the handle of the spoon with the tip of a bradawl. Screw in small hooks (these can be bought in haberdashery shops or on fabric counters in big stores). Make two more holes on the opposite side of the handle and screw in two rings. Tie ribbon through the rings and the spoon keyholder is ready to be hung up from a nail. If you like, make the spoon like a strange animal by putting an eye and a mouth on the bowl part. Cut the eye and mouth from felt or use coloured paper stick-on shapes. You could decorate the whole spoon with stick-on shapes if you liked.

Mrs Teaslemouse

Mothers, aunts, sisters and grandmothers are going to love having a Mrs Teaslemouse for a mascot. There is very little sewing to do and you need only a very pretty piece of material and some lace.
Making the body Look for a really big teasle in the garden or in the hedgerows. Cut it off just under the head. This is for the body. Now look for a small teasle for the head. If you cannot find one, you may have to cut a big teasle in half.

You will need two cloves for the eyes and one for the nose. If you cannot find whole cloves, use beads or used matchstick heads. Glue the eyes and nose to the pointed end of the smaller

teasle. Glue the small teasle on top of the larger as in *diagram 4*. (You may have to cut the point off the larger teasle to get the head to perch steadily and not fall off.)
The clothes Measure from Mrs Teaslemouse's neck to the table top. Cut a piece of the material to this measurement by 20cm (8in). If you can borrow a pair of pinking shears, cut round the hem and down the two sides. Thread a needle and double the thread, tying a knot in the ends. Work running stitches right along the top edge. Put the dress round the mouse's neck and pull up the gathers until the material fits round the mouse's neck. Tie the knot and the other end together, cutting off the needle first. Now to put in the two little hands. The hands are 'leaves' pulled from a fircone. Cut two little slits in the front of the dress and glue in the hands.
Making the mobcap The little mobcap is made last of all. Using a cup or a glass, draw round it to make a circle about 65mm (2½in) across on a piece of material. Cut the circle out (use pinking shears if you have them). Sew a piece of lace all round the edge of the circle. Thread a big-eyed needle with a piece of shirring elastic. Work running stitches round the circle 12mm (½in) from the edge. Draw it up to fit the mouse's head and then knot the ends.

For fun, present the mouse in her own glass jar. Wash a jar and dry it thoroughly. Put the mouse inside. Cut a circle of fabric (the same as the dress) 25mm (1in) larger all round than the jar top. Put the fabric circle on for a lid, holding it on with a rubber band.

4

Index

Air-dry flowers and herbs, to 28, 32
Animals:
    fabric 47, 55, 63, 68, 70-1
    from a teasle 92, 95
    knitted 90-1
    papier mâché 80, 94
Appliqué, string and card 81
Appliqué cushion 58
Aprons:
    embroidered 20-1
    hostess 24-5

Bags:
    herb 93
    money 54
    moth 35
Baskets, baby 17
Belt, plaited leather 64
Bookmarks 93
Borax, drying flowers in 28, 30
Bouquet, paper 74
Bouquet garni balls 35
Bowls, papier mâché 80
Bows, to make 84
Boxes:
    to cover 73
    sewing 26
    work 14, 15
    to wrap 84
Brushes:
    for découpage 79
    for painting stones 44
    for stencilling 42

Cable stitch 14, 15
Candlesticks, papier mâché 80
Candlewax printing techniques
    39-40
Canvaswork pincushion 22
Card case, leather 64
Cards, greetings 82-3
Carnation, paper 76
Car wash mitt 67
Cases:
    card 64
    crayon 56
    map 66-7
    pencil 56-7
    pyjama 70-1
Cat, doorstep 63
Cat cushion 63
Chevron stitch 14
Chrysanthemum, ribbon 84
Clamshell patchwork 12-13
Coffeepot cosy 24
Collage 31, 83
Containers, gift 85
Cover:
    for needlebook 14, 15
    for plant pot 81
    for tissue box 73
Coverlets:
    doll's 53
    patchwork 11
Cradle, doll's 52-3
Cretan stitch 55
Crochet 86
Cross stitch 21
Cushions:
    animal 47, 63
    appliqué 58
    cat 63

covers for 25
elephant 47
fancy 24
owl 47
ribbon 58-9
woven 58-9
Cutouts, decorating with 84

Daisy, ribbon 84
Daisy Mae rag doll 18-19
Découpage 78-9
Desiccant, drying flowers with a
    28, 29
Dog, sleepy 68
Dolls:
    knitted 89
    miniature 8
    rag 18-19
Doorstep cat 63
Dressing table set 73

Eggs, papier mâché 85
Elephant, knitted 90-1
Elephant cushion 47
Embroidery:
    on apron 20-1
    on canvas 22
    stitches 14

Fabric 54-63
    animals 47, 55, 63, 68, 70-1
    boxes 26
    collage 83
    for smocking 15
    for wrapping gifts 85
Fan, lavender 34
Felt 54-7
    collage 83
    pencil and crayon cases 56-7
    thimble pips 55
Flower pictures 31
Flower press 30, 31
Flower sachets 34
Flowers 28-35
    dried, as collage 83
    to dry 28, 30, 32
    paper 74-6
    pressed 30-1
Frame, fabric picture 73

Gift wrapping 84-5
Greetings cards 82-3

Hammers 48
Handkerchiefs, gifts made from
    24-5
Herbs 32-5
    to dry 32
Hollyhock, paper 74, 76
Honeycomb stitch 14, 15

Immortelles 28
Initialling gifts 85

Keyholder, spoon 95
Key ring tag 67
Knitting 89-91

Lavender fan 34
Leather gifts 64-7
Letter cards, to 83

Map case 66-7
Masking tape 39, 42
Masks, papier mâché 80
Matchbox bureau 60-1
Matchboxes, fabric-covered 60
Measure, wall 48-9
Mrs Teaslemouse 95

Mitts:
    car wash 67
    polishing 67
Money bags 54
Morning glories, paper 76
Moth bags 35
Mouse:
    paperweight 92
    from a teasle 92, 95
    thimble pip 55

Naming gifts 85
Needlebook, smocked 14, 15
Needlecase, apple-shaped 92-3
Needlework 8-15

Owl cushion 47

Paint, to:
    tinware 36-7
    wood 39, 40-1
Paints:
    acrylic 38, 42
    for découpage 79
    enamel 37
    gloss 39, 40-1
    oil 42
    poster 39, 42
    for stencilling 42
    for stones 44, 45
    water-based 42
Papercrafts 74-7
Paperweights:
    mouse 92
    stone 45
Papier mâché 80-1
    eggs 85
    savings pig 80, 94
Patchwork:
    clamshell 12-13
    crazy 11
Patchwork coverlet 11
Patchwork pincushion 94-5
Pencil case 56-7
Pencil folder 57
Pencil holders 56-7, 93
Perfume pots 35
Petals, ribbon 84
Picture frame, fabric 73
Pictures on stones 44-5
Pig, savings 80, 94
Pillows:
    doll's 53
    lacy 24
Pincushions:
    canvaswork 22
    patchwork 94-5
Pips, thimble 55
Polishing mitt 67
Pomander ball 35
Poppy, paper 76
Pot cover, papier mâché 81
Pot-pourris 32, 34
Pots, perfume 35
Pressing flowers 30-1
Punches, nail 48
Pyjama case, bunny 70-1

Rabbit thimble pip 55
Rack, spice 50-1
Rag doll 18-19
Ribbon:
    chrysanthemum 84
    cushions 58-9
    daisy 84
    petals 84
    weaving 58-9
Roses:
    to paint 37

paper 74
in pot-pourri 34
Rosette, easy 84
Rosette bows 84

Sachets:
    flower 34
    ribbon 34
Saws 48
Screwdrivers 48
Sewing box 26
Shawl, crocheted 86
Skirt, smocked 15
Smocking 14-15
Soft toys 47, 68, 90-1
Spice rack 50-1
Spices in pot-pourris 32
Spoon keyholder 95
Stem stitch 14, 15
Stencils, decorating with 42
Stitches, smocking and
    embroidery 14, 15, 21
Stone painting 44-5
Surforms 48
Sweet Sue 89

Table cloth, handkerchief 25
Teacosy, clamshell 12-13
Thimble pips 55
Tinware, to paint 36-7
Tissue box cover 73
Tissue paper collage 83
Toys:
    papier mâché 80, 94
    soft 47, 68, 70-1, 90-1
Transfers 39, 45
Tray, papier mâché 80
Tree, jewelled 77

Waste bin, to cover 73
Wheelbrace 48
Woodcraft 48-53
Work box, smocked 14, 15
Wrapping, gift 84-5

Acknowledgments

The publishers would like to thank the following for their contributions to this book:

Designers: Jan Deller, Maxine Fitter, Valerie Jackson, Etrenne Joll, Mary Clark Maxwell, Stephanie Morgan, Jean & Angela Mott, Mary Pilcher, Lynette Merlin Syme.

Photography by J&P Coats Limited 23; Dylon International Limited 46-47; John Gill 13, 27, 58; Bob Golden 1-3, 30-31, 34-35, 54, 56-57, 59, 65, 71, 84; A. P. Green 29; Valerie Jackson 75, 77; Barry Jell 25 below, 43, 49-53, 66, 67, 78-79, 80-81, 83, 92-95; John Ledger 6-9, 14, 28, 36-39, 44, 45, 60, 62, 68-69, 88-89; A. Lewis 55; Syndication International Limited 24, 25 above, 32-33.

Artwork by Marion Mills and Norman Sherrington.